PRAISE FOR "INSIDE SALES MANAGEMENT"

If you're committed to success—whether it be in sales or management—learn these strategies by heart. This is nothing less than a course in the psychology of business, and it should be required reading in business schools.

—*Vic Mallen, Vice-president of Sales, Patton Solutions*

This book should be required for every sales manager! Mark Wilensky clearly explains how to understand and grow the people you manage. It's about time somebody put it all together in one volume!

—*Robin Domeniconi, President, Time Inc. Media Group*

To really serve your clients, you have to know how they think. In this book Mark Wilensky provides you with the codes to unlock your customers, your salespeople and what's happening between them. Even if you implement only a fraction of his strategies, you'll see a dramatic upward trend in sales revenues!

—*Steve Sachs, Publisher, Real Simple Magazine*

Getting inside the mind of salespeople—and clients—is the key to successful sales management, and that is exactly what this book does. I gained dozens of invaluable insights into how to motivate people, buyers and sellers, and you will too!

—*Don Combs, president, Colonial Equipment Co*

This is the first book I've seen that clearly describes how to grow people! Mark Wilensky's unique insights into what makes salespeople successful and what holds them back should be required reading for anyone hoping to develop a successful sales organization.

—*Ian Scott, CEO and President, Bauer Ad Sales*

Managers—If you're tired of not meeting your forecasts, this is the book you've been waiting for. The stories and examples make this vital knowledge come alive. I've read the chapter on becoming an all star coach three times, and I'm not through learning from it.

—Richard Daniels, Vice President of Sales, PDI

At last—an understanding of salespeople, and how to ensure better sales results, all written in a style that any sales manager can readily grasp. Everyone with a stake in their company's success will thank you for presenting the strategies in this book.

—Charlie Browning, Publisher, New Homes Guide

I've read many books on the sales management process, and Mark Wilensky deals very effecively with the underlying causes of success and failure in managing sales. He demonstrates how to easily build a dynamic sales force that will exceed company goals. These insights will definitely increase your sales!

—Frank Wintroub, president, The Rose Company

There is nothing more important in managing the sales process than understanding the people involved...salespeople and clients —their expectations, their fears, and how to deal with them. Wilensky's book gets inside the minds of buyers and sellers, and managers will benefit tremendously from this penetrating knowledge.

—Gib Dickey, President, Housing Guides of America

Mark Wilensky has helped us double sales year after year, and I'm delighted that he has collected his strategies in this volume, which truly leads you inside sales management.

—Don Alducin, founder and CEO of HJ Ford

Inside
Sales Management

Secrets to Growing Salespeople and Sales

Mark Wilensky

1st WORLD
PUBLISHING

Inside Sales Management

MARK WILENSKY

© Mark Wilensky 2006

Published by 1stWorld Publishing
1100 North 4th St. Fairfield, Iowa 52556
tel: 641-209-5000 • fax: 641-209-3001
web: www.1stworldpublishing.com

First Edition

LCCN: 2006935104
SoftCover ISBN: 1-59540-884-3
HardCover ISBN: 1-59540-883-5
eBook ISBN: 1-59540-885-1

This material has been written and published solely for educational purposes. The author and the publisher shall have neither liability or responsibility to any person or entity with respect to any loss, damage or injury caused or alleged to be caused directly or indirectly by the information contained in this book.

The characters and events described in this text are intended to entertain and teach rather than present an exact factual history of real people or events.

TABLE OF CONTENTS

Part II: Sales Psychology

Acknowledgments

First of all, I want to thank my friend and colleague Bill Cates for his suggestion that I write a book on sales psychology. Eric Berne's groundbreaking work in what became transactional analysis underlies the basic structure of this book. Sue Collier has provided more than professional editing; she guided me through the mazes confronting any new author.

Over the past 20 years, there have been hundreds of company owners and managers who trusted enough to allow me to consult with and train their staffs, enabling me to develop and validate all the strategies and concepts in this book. I recognize that it's a privilege to be able to help companies and individuals grow.

Finally, my wife Susan has never stopped giving or encouraging me. I could have no better partner in business or in life.

Introduction

James sells for a leading financial services company. He's polite, sincere, and personable-the kind of individual everybody wants to see succeed. You'd even be happy if your daughter brought him home for Thanksgiving! After five months on the job, both he and his manager are frustrated because he's not closing enough business, in spite of the fact that he gets plenty of appointments. His prospects like him, but they rarely become clients.

Now consider Bill—a mediocre salesman at a restaurant supply company. After seven years his book of business consists of customers who obviously like him. But his average dollar sale is just that—average—and it's not growing. Bill always has reasons: One large account has a corporate mandate to spread the business around; another major customer is buying from his cousin; a third account is always promising more business next quarter. Bill does well enough to stay in the game, but he never seems to win. You are more frustrated with his performance than he is.

And there's Tamara, a mercurial sales rep for a high-tech firm. An outstanding quarter of sales revenue is invariably followed by two or three poor months, then a struggle to get back in the upper third of the sales force. At the end of the year, her numbers are better than average, but her manager thinks, *What a waste of talent! If she was more consistent she could become a top producer.*

If you are an experienced sales manager, these salespeople sound all too familiar. You've probably tried numerous approaches with varying degrees of success. And like most managers, you may still be trying to "figure these people out" so you can help them become more successful. I'm going to share with you some profound insights about salespeople that will enable you to get your people growing personally and professionally. Of course as they grow, your revenues and bottom line grow as well—along with your reputation as a successful manager and the satisfaction you get from your career. This is why I wrote this book.

After 30 years of selling, managing, training, coaching, and studying people who sell, I'm excited about sharing what I've learned. A word of caution here: After working with me for a while, my clients frequently tell me, "You know, much of what you've taught me is common sense. It's really effective, but I should have known this stuff all along!"

I always agree. But it was Mark Twain who may have first stated publicly what we all know: *Common sense isn't so common anymore!*

Let's begin with the insights that are fundamental to the pages that follow:

1. Both sales and sales management are largely psychological.

2. When you understand the *why* and the *how* behind the *what*, you can motivate people to change—salespeople, prospects, and clients.

3. The recipe for successful selling is equal parts sales psychology, sales technique, and guts. As a sales trainer for

many years, I can say with confidence that technique is the least important part.

4. The goal of selling and managing is to identify and close gaps for your clients.

5. If you manage salespeople, you're in the growth business, which is not the same as the social rehabilitation business.

6. If you want to be successful in growing your salespeople, you have to treat the causes of the problems and not just the symptoms.

7. You yourself must be willing to change and grow.

The year 2006 is the 100th anniversary of Italian economist Vilfredo Pareto's observation that 20 percent of Italy's adult population owned 80 percent of the country's wealth. This later became the foundation for the 80/20 rule, known as the Pareto Principle. It often goes like this: 80 percent of the business is produced by 20 percent of the salespeople. What you will learn from the following pages will equip you change this formula to 80/80. Your total revenues will increase dramatically, while 80 percent (up from 20 percent) of your sales staff will produce 80 percent of your business. Your top producers will get even better, your middle group will show tremendous improvement, and your weakest people in most cases will be left behind.

Before the last chapter you will have solved the challenges that James, Bill, and Tamara present. You'll also know how best to grow each of the people on your staff.

This book is not a sales manager's handbook or encyclopedia; these texts are already available in bookstores. Instead I've chosen to focus on the most difficult but common sales management challenges that stand between you and greater success. You won't find chapters on how to give an annual review or how to run a sales meeting. What you will find are chapters on how to deal with excuses, how to reduce a salesperson's need for approval; how to become an expert coach; and how to recruit, hire, and bring new salespeople up to speed—all while maintaining your sanity.

In each chapter I've highlighted some *Key Thoughts* for you to review and return to. For managers who also sell, and for those of you who aren't yet in management, I've included specific strategies for you under the heading *If You Sell*. These points include actions items any salesperson can apply immediately to get better results. In writing this book I've taken the easy (lazy?) way out by referring to salespeople as either he or she without going through the extra effort of including both genders. If I've offended anyone, I trust you will find enough value in the following pages to forgive me.

Experiment with what you learn as you go; don't wait until you've finished the last chapter before trying something. You'll find too many new concepts and strategies to incorporate at one time anyway.

Part Two of this book deals with sales psychology, specifically the psychology of selling, buying, prospecting, resistance, and persuasion. Regardless of whether you sell or manage, these insights and strategies will give you a decided edge in every client interaction. These chapters are designed to make you and your staff better presenters, better negotiators, and better closers.

Finally, I'd like to pass along an observation about salespeople who excel: Successful people have formed the habit of regularly doing what less successful people are unwilling to do.

Your top salespeople probably aren't more intelligent than your mediocre performers. Their success comes from the desire, courage, effort, and understanding they employ with their customers. As you learn why your salespeople perform as they do and how to help them grow, you'll all have greater success. And isn't that why you go to work every day?

Part I

Sales Management Psychology

Chapter 1

The Psychology of Salespeople

Who's Inside You?

Psychology, one of the "soft" sciences, deals with mental processes and behavior. Because you manage salespeople, you can add *social scientist* to your job description; you study their actions to improve their results. I'm going to take your focus deeper, into their thoughts and feelings, so you can bring about positive change more quickly. Whether you sell, manage, or do both jobs, knowing the how and why behind your clients' thoughts and words allows you to influence what they will do. If you're like most managers, you've moved up the corporate ladder by succeeding in sales. You've had to make the transition from hunter to farmer, and your growth now comes from getting more production out of your salespeople. You are now an account manager, and your sales staff has become your accounts. You need to become an expert on each of them.

In the 1960s, psychiatrist Eric Berne gained fame and fortune from his development of transactional analysis and its insights into how and why people act as they do. His best-selling book *Games People Play*, published in 1964, offered insights into human behavior that have particular relevance today in understanding the motivations and fears confronting salespeople—and even sales managers. The book gathered a wide following among psychologists and the general public.

Inside each of us, Berne said, there is a Parent, an Adult, and a Child. He called these mini-personalities ego states. According to Berne, when you acted in a parental manner, you were in your Parent ego state. When you behaved in an intellectual, rational, unemotional way, you were acting in your Adult ego state. And when emotions formed the basis of your actions, you were in your Child ego state. Think of the Child as the feeler, the Adult as the thinker, and the Parent as the one saying, "I/you should/shouldn't." You can also imagine the three ego states as points of view: The Parent sees things as they should be; the Adult sees things as they are; the Child see things as it wants them to be.

The messages and information—valid or not—came with our first experiences in life. We learned when to laugh and cry, when (and how) to judge others, not to touch a hot stove, to look both ways before crossing the street, and so on. We also may have learned not to talk to strangers (Think this might play a role in call reluctance among salespeople?), always to give a straight answer, never to tell lies, that certain groups of people are lazy, clever, not to be trusted (Salespeople?), and so on. The messages are all there, and many of them influence what we believe and how we act today. Keep in mind that we are all a mixture of these ego states, but we function from only one of them at any given moment. (It's been postulated that psychotic individuals actually function simultaneously from more than one ego state, but I'm assuming this has little relevance to your salespeople.)

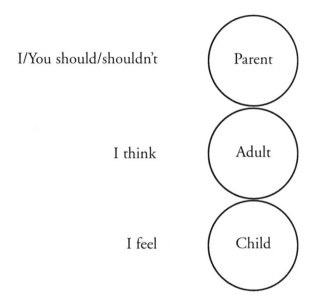

I/You should/shouldn't   Parent

I think   Adult

I feel   Child

The diagram above should make this clearer. Berne explained that initially, when we were born, we consisted of just one ego state—the Child. And like every human before and since, we could feel basically one of two ways—OK or not-OK. OKness is the preferred way of feeling about ourselves because it means good, confident, enthusiastic, comfortable, secure. Not-OK feelings include insecure, anxious, worried, tense, frightened. You get the picture. Not surprisingly, when given the choice we will choose situations that provide us with feelings of OKness over not-OKness. In sales and sales management, this is a key factor on the roads leading to success, mediocrity, or failure.

In fact, if we feel intensely not-OK, a stress response kicks in—we want to fight or run away. This fight-or-flight response, although useful in prehistoric times when we were faced with daily life-or-death situations, isn't as applicable today. As a result, billions of dollars are spent on medicines for ulcers, depression, and other forms of anxiety. In our society it has become acceptable to medicate not-OK feelings so we can regain, if only temporarily, OK feelings about ourselves. And in a selling situation, if a salesperson says or does something to generate not-OK feelings in his customer, that customer will want to end the meeting or even the relationship. Being all too sensitive to this possibility, many salespeople don't address situations, problems, or client objections head on for fear of "blowing the sale."

Let's consider the Child ego state and its role in OKness. More than anything, the Child just wants to have fun. It seeks pleasure and usually avoids work because—let's face it—if it was fun, they wouldn't call it work! The Child tends to be self-centered and spontaneous. Berne coined the phrase "feeding your Child" to describe how we reward ourselves with fun behavior, sometimes even when we should be working. Does this sound like any of your salespeople?

Our Parent ego state tells us, *You gotta go to work.* We're getting paid, so it's the responsible and equitable thing to do. The Adult computes, *If I go to work, I get paid.* Then I can pay my bills and afford a new car. If I don't go to work, I will get in trouble and could lose my job. The factors are clearly in favor of this decision.

The questions are, *Which ego state is in charge? Which one determines behavior?*

Actually, it varies from person to person and moment to moment. You probably know people who always seem to be in their Parent ego state. They're the designated driver, the timekeeper, the one who reminds you about the important things you've left undone. What they lack in spontaneity, they make up for by getting all kinds of jobs done. These people often add up the *shoulds* they took care of each day, and then either feel a sense of satisfaction (OKness), or dissatisfaction (not-OKness). They see themselves as responsible and act accordingly. They're Parents!

Who do you think depends most on the Parent? Naturally, it's the Child—the playful expert at rationalizing why it's not necessary to go to work now. The Child looks to the Parent for approval, for strokes, for reassurance, and even for a reality check. Transactional analysis (TA) folks tell us that the Child is actually made up of three parts:

1. The Natural Child—wants to play and experience pleasure—now.

2. The Rebellious Child (also called the Little Professor) is intuitive, manipulative, even shrewd. This is the part of us that figures out how to call in to work sick so we can play golf.

3. The Adapted Child—changes its behavior to gain acceptance and approval, to fit in.

(See diagram below)

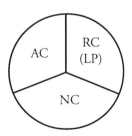

Note that each aspect of the Child ego state has its strengths and weaknesses. As with most things in life, balance and moderation are key. You don't want to work with somebody who is never serious and is always playing around (the Natural Child), but you also like people who know how to have fun and enjoy a good joke. You don't want to deal with somebody who's always manipulating you (Little Professor), but you like seeing a salesperson who can manipulate (you might be more comfortable with the term "orchestrate" here) the sales call so your company is better positioned to win the business.

Now let's turn to the Adapted Child. From the earliest stages of our lives, we all have need for approval. Initially, most of us got it from our mothers, and we felt loved—the ultimate OK feeling! If we didn't get enough (or any) love from Mom, we felt not-OK. Depending on the actual circumstances and how we perceived and dealt with them, we could still feel very not-OK about ourselves years later. Many adults are still looking for approval and acceptance—OKness from others—as a means of self-validation. (Note: Don't blame your mother; it's probably not accurate, and definitely won't help.) They may avoid doing or saying anything that might upset others. But this is a very one-sided view of the Adapted Child. It's also the part of our personality that reminds us to keep quiet during the sermon in church, to say "please" and "thank you." It enables us to fit in, which is beneficial in many situations.

It might be helpful to view the Child ego state generally as the home of four basic feelings:

1. Glad
2. Mad
3. Sad
4. Scared

We could list many subclasses of feelings, but let's keep it simple. Have you noticed that three of these four are negative, not-OK feelings? Hmm…three out of four. Those aren't very good odds for feeling good if we're in our Child state, especially when at work our playful side is rarely appropriate.

☞ Key Thought

❖ If your salesperson is in his Child ego state, there's a good chance he's already in or headed for not-OK territory. Emotionally involved, he may not see things objectively and will unlikely have control of the situation.

By now you probably recognize some of your salespeople in these descriptions. Consider a salesperson with an exceedingly strong Adapted Child—he has high need for approval. How comfortable will he be hearing *No!* from a prospect or client? Think this might have something to do with how effective this person is when prospecting or when closing a sale? (More on this in the pages ahead.)

Before continuing our discussion of the Child ego state, let's revisit the Parent. Berne tells us that there are actually two parts to the Parent: Critical Parent and Nurturing Parent. If you've ever had a manager with an overly strong Critical Parent, you remember this person as very judgmental and critical. You may have feared being called into his office. There are likely not many fond memories.

Years ago I worked with a client who was all Critical Parent. As I was trying to teach him how to manage more effectively, Gerald would complain to me, "Look, I already pay these people more than the industry average. Now you're telling me I have to be nice to them as well?"

Think he had trouble keeping staff? There was an imbalance, and what was lacking was the other part of his Parent—what Berne referred to as Nurturing Parent, which gives strokes and provides caring, comfort, and friendship. Gerald's Critical Parent generated substantial not-OK feelings in the Child ego states of his employees. Naturally, they didn't enjoy feeling not-OK, so they quit.

People who live mostly in their Parent

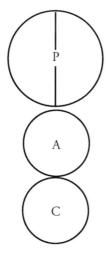

"Shoulds" and "ought tos" drive him; he can lack spontaneity.

My wife Susan is the classic Nurturing Parent. Not coincidentally, she has a master's degree in psychiatric nursing, has also worked in pediatric nursing, and is currently a bereavement counselor for Hospice. She has a well-earned reputation as a wonderful caregiver and loyal friend who's always "there" for you in your time of need. (Carole King must have had her in mind with her song "You've Got a Friend.") If you have salespeople like this, their clients love them. In fact, these people can excel as account managers, as well as in sales service and customer care. They don't offend anyone. Do they make good closers? Not usually, because they are so focused on the relationship that they shy away from any action that might seem to threaten it, like asking for a buying decision. For decades the life insurance industry has recruited schoolteachers into the industry, because they were articulate and caring. This is true, as far as it goes, and I know several extremely successful producers in the industry who made the shift from a teaching career. I've also seen far more former schoolteachers who couldn't make the transition successfully, and usually one insurmountable obstacle was their super-strong Nurturing Parent. They made many friends but not enough clients.

Whether you sell or manage, if you have a strong Nurturing Parent, people probably like you, enjoy working with (and for) you, and remain loyal to you. If you have a strong Critical Parent you get results in spite of your "people skills," not because of them. If you've ever taken a class in effective parenting, the instructor probably explained these concepts and advised you to communicate with your kids using your Nurturing Parent, unless it was an emergency and they were in danger. And this is great advice you can always use to advantage—unless you're tired, frustrated, not feeling well, overwhelmed, pressed for time—hey, this sounds a lot like a full-time parent, doesn't it? There's often a gap between the ideal situation and the real world.

Effective managers know when and how to use their Critical Parent. With any position of authority, the Critical Parent is always there, implied, just waiting to come into play. Successful managers find ways to use their Adult instead, because they don't want their salespeople retreating into their Child, where learning can't occur.

☞ Key Thought

❖ If you want your staff to grow, they need to stay out of their Child, and you need to stay out of your Critical Parent.

Caution: Just because a salesperson was born more than 21 years ago is no guarantee that he's in his Adult. Child behavior is all too evident. Salespeople in their Child are the ones

❖ who are always trying to impress you (and others), due to their need for approval,

❖ who can't help taking shortcuts, even when it's clear they shouldn't,

❖ who consistently exaggerate in their activity reports and forecasts,

❖ who knock on your door to tell you whenever they have a victory, no matter how small,

❖ who just can't resist telling you about other employees who mess up,

❖ who take delight in the failures and frustrations of others,

❖ who get their emotional needs met in front of a client by talking too much and trying to impress him,

❖ who continuously take the customer's or prospect's side in any negotiation,

❖ who spend too much time establishing friendships and relationships with customers in the hopes that this will lead to business, only later to give you reasons why the business won't come until next quarter, and

❖ who blame the client for being too pushy, demanding too much, failing to appreciate the value you offer, going with the competition.

All these examples of Child behavior can be part of your day. Because they can lead to frustration and job dissatisfaction, I'll show you how to manage all of them.

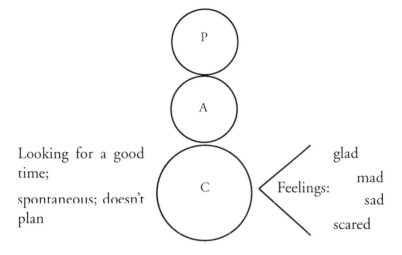

Looking for a good time; spontaneous; doesn't plan

Feelings: glad mad sad scared

☞ **Key Thought**

❖ All growth occurs from within the Adult ego state. Don't expect your salesperson to grow when he's in his Child.

This is logical because the Child is so emotionally involved it can't or refuses to see the big picture. The Child has no objectivity, no sense of perspective. If you try to correct somebody in his Child, don't expect to see changes in behavior. What you usually get are excuses. I've covered this in chapter 6.

On the other hand, if you have salespeople

❖ who constantly criticize and find fault with others,

❖ who find themselves telling what their customers are doing wrong,

❖ who have trouble retaining clients,

❖ who find themselves helping customers with non-business problems, and

❖ whose shoulders are constantly wet with everyone else's tears, then you're dealing with the Parent behavior-Critical (the first three bullets) or Nurturing (the last two).

Years ago Terri sold training programs for me, and she was the best I've ever seen at uncovering information and feelings from prospects in the first meeting. The problem was that she would come back from these calls with information such as "Sharon is an adult child of an alcoholic," or "Norm is having trouble in his marriage." Great stuff, if you were writing a soap opera. Not so great if you were trying to sell sales training.

What was going on here? Well, several things, but most importantly, Terri was such a Nurturing Parent that prospects felt completely safe in opening up to her. She bonded quickly and generated enough trust to open a discussion about virtually anything. Unfortunately, she wasn't closing business. I suspect many prospects who had told her their private stories later regretted or felt embarrassed about it, and weren't looking forward to seeing her again. It took three months of conversations with me—and the realization that she wasn't making any money—for her to learn how to use her exceptional skill to help prospects discover they needed our training programs.

I found it striking that once she started using her Nurturing Parent more effectively, I stopped hearing about her prospects' personal lives. Terri learned how to remain focused on her business agenda, and she closed business regularly. I'm sure she still had the ability to uncover personal stuff, but she no longer had the need. Terri's psychological (in her Child) needs stopped overshadowing her financial (in her Adult) needs. Like all professionals she stayed in her Adult to think strategically, moved into her Nurturing Parent to ask questions in a nonthreatening manner, and kept her Child out of the scenario until it was time to celebrate.

Incidentally, this is the same procedure used in every profession, not just sales. Psychiatrists invest years in learning how to avoid become emotionally involved (the Child) so they can evaluate clearly and objectively (the Adult). They learn how to elicit information from their patients/clients in a way that befriends (the Nurturing Parent) instead of demanding or threatening (Critical Parent), and this creates trust and openness. Engineers, architects, accountants, dentists—all professionals work from their Adult so they can perform at their best.

TA advocates warn that when you go on a sales call, you should leave your Child in the car. So how often should you be in your Adult when selling? How about when you're managing? Because the Adult behavior is objective, rational, logical, analytical, and contemplative-you might find that tiring after a while. And if you were always in your Adult, others would eventually find you tiring. Many customers don't enjoy dealing with salespeople who live in their Adult. Customers want to have fun and be entertained too.

Who are these people who live in their Adult ego state? What do they sell? Well, many are engineers—if not in terms of profession, at least by personality—they are analytical, often in love with details and technology. They may prefer to work on tasks or solve problems rather than manage relationships. Their job description has evolved through the years from engineer/product specialist to sales engineer to salesperson. They thrive when selling to other engineers because they speak the same language and enjoy analyzing their products.

Although many customers find these salespeople uninteresting and even tedious in meetings, their knowledge and authority commands respect. In short, they have their place in the sales world, but you need to be sure they're a good fit with their product and customer. With the sprouting of so many technology businesses in the 1990s, increasingly more of these Adult ego state folks have found a comfortable role in professional sales.

People who live in their Adult:

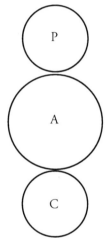

Always thinking, intellectualizing, analyzing wondering how things work, asking why, gathering data, calculating, evaluating

There's much more you can learn about Parent, Adult, and Child ego states, but perhaps the most important thing to keep in mind is that they are always in play. And remembering this will help you determine what's going on with your salespeople.

If You Sell

It's easy to identify ego states in other people, but more difficult to see them in ourselves. In order to determine what ego state you are in (or were in five minutes ago when you were speaking to a client), answer the following questions:

1. If I had to choose one, was I thinking (Adult) or feeling

(Child) just now?

2. If I was in a "feeling mode," which one of the following best describes my feeling-glad, mad, sad, or scared?

3. How emotionally involved was I during this client interaction?

4. If I was thinking, what did I observe about my client? What did I learn?

5. Overall, did I feel more OK or not—OK during this sales call?

6. Was I more focused on my client (in my Parent or in my Adult) or on myself (in my Child)?

The last question gets to the bottom line about what was happening and who was in control. Much of the work I do with salespeople is helping them to focus—and stay focused—on the client or prospect because obviously this is where "all the action is taking place." In the chapters on the psychology of selling and buying, you'll see how it's done.

☞ Key Thoughts

❖ Do you have "Adults" trying to sell products and services that require a lot of enthusiasm and emotion? (Bad idea.)

❖ Do you have a Child trying to sell very technical products and services to Adults? (May not be a great fit.)

❖ If you have a salesperson that ends us arguing with clients, he needs to understand that Critical Parent is showing in order to improve his relationships.

Chapter 2

Managing the Adapted Child

Needing Love, Getting Respect

We each have a Child inside us. In some of us, it's strong and active—even to the point of overshadowing the Parent and Adult ego states. In the workplace it's

❖ the Adult who goes to work, at least in part because

❖ the Parent says it's the responsible thing to do, in spite of the fact that

❖ the Child wants to play instead.

These three ego states make up every personality. Multiply this by several times and you have a sales staff. It's no wonder sales management is so often compared to parenting.

Let's understand the Child in more detail. Berne says the Child can be divided into three subdivisions:

1. The Natural Child

(a) Is playful

(b) Finds humor and fun in many situations

(c) Causes problems in meetings when he's cutting up

(d) Needs to balance fun with (more) work

(e) Doesn't enjoy activities like planning and prioritizing

2. The Rebellious Child (also called the Little Professor)

(a) Manipulates others—colleagues, management, clients, and prospects

(b) Looks for shortcuts

(c) Bends the rules to gain advantage

(d) Is creative

(e) Is intuitive

(f) May exaggerate on call reports and business forecasts

(g) Can tell you what he thinks you want to hear

(h) Can take shortcuts, concerned about explanations and apologies only later, if at all

3. The Adapted Child

(a) Has a high need for approval, acceptance, praise, and love

(b) Often looks for this approval from prospects and clients

(c) Seeks approval from you

(d) Tends to give away too much, too soon in negotiations

(e) Often spends time negotiating/debating with you on behalf of clients

(f) Has trouble justifying "your" pricing to his clients and himself

(g) May spend time trying to solve problems for clients

without charging

(h) Can be high maintenance, taking up too much of your time

(i) Has a hard time delivering bad news and telling others *No!*

(Remember James from the introduction? We've described him above in greater detail. In the following pages you'll learn how to help him grow, both personally and professionally.)

Exercise

List your salespeople below, and next to their names write down the number/letter of each description above that fits. I'll start the list with a hypothetical example—Karen Watkins. She has consistently lower profit margins to her sales, frequently asks you for special considerations for his customers, and needs to tell you whenever something good is happening. If your cell phone rings, it's probably her.

Karen Watkins: 3b, 3c, 3d, 3h, 3i

Your salespeople:

1.

2.

3.

4.

5.

6.

As you view your sales staff in the context of these descriptions, you'll have a clearer picture of what your real management challenges are. The list contains only the consequences of certain ego states dominating your salespeople's actions. The longer the list, of course, the bigger the problem. But before you get too disheartened, remember that you can't manage consequences; they've already happened. You have to deal with the cause, which in Karen's case is that she's stuck in her Child looking for approval. The old country and western song about looking for love in "all the wrong places" fits Karen perfectly.

My friend Bill, an outstanding neuropsychologist with a national reputation, has many profound insights. Here's one of my favorites:

All behavior has a positive intent.

It sounds good, but what does it mean? Simply put, it means that people do what they think will bring them happiness and pleasure. A corollary would be that people tend to avoid doing what brings them unhappiness or pain. In TA lingo, people want to feel OK about themselves, and they avoid feeling not—OK whenever possible. In the sixties, we used to say, "If it feels good, do it." (I guess, if it doesn't feel good, don't do it, which is probably why so many young people dropped out of society for a while instead of going to work.)

But wait, you ask: What about people who shoot heroin into their veins? What about people who stay in painful relationships? What about people who listen to Tom Jones's songs?

Drug addicts obviously act for short-term pleasure, in spite of the long-term pain they're creating for themselves and others who care about them. Individuals stuck in painful relationships often find an unknown future more painful to contemplate than a hurtful present. And for those who swoon to a Tom Jones song, that's your pleasure. Because this gives me pain, I avoid them at every opportunity.

An old joke comes to mind:

Masochist: Hit me!

Sadist: No!

Pleasure and pain, like beauty, can lie in the eyes of the beholder.

Now that you've listed your salespeople, it's time to consider which symptoms are most costly, to them and you. Taken together they can spell problems, or even disaster, so let's formulate corrective action.

Remember that you're in the growth business. As your people grow, so do your revenues and profits. You also know that an individual's professional growth isn't going to far outpace his personal growth. Consequently, your leverage in growing your people is to help them grow personally. This includes helping them outgrow their fears.

In spite of President George W. Bush's federal education program No Child Left Behind, I'm convinced that real growth on your sales staff will come from just that—leaving the Child behind when it comes to professional selling.

🖙 Key Thoughts

❖ Transactional Analysis describes all growth as taking place in the Adult ego state. (It's the only ego state that's still recording new messages.)

Therefore, if a salesperson is in her Child, she can't learn or grow. This means there will be no change. And you will be frustrated.

If You Sell

❖ List those clients and prospects that you find threatening or intimidating, even if only a little.

❖ Now consider what each one says and does that causes you to fall into your Child ego state. This part won't be easy for you. In some instances they may not be doing anything, at least consciously. They may have no idea that you feel threatened or intimidated. Even if they are aware of it, they may not believe they're responsible for it.

❖ There's really only one logical (Adult) conclusion you can draw here: Most of the time you are doing this to yourself. This is great news because if you're doing it, you can stop!

❖ When you have these feelings—and it can happen even when one of these names pops up in your daily schedule on your computer—ask yourself the following:

—Do they know I am feeling this way in relation to them right now?

—Do they care?

—How would I like to feel whenever I think of this person?

—I'll try it, right now.

—Remember, this is a test. Only a test. No one is looking or listening to how I feel. Nobody cares. No one will notice. Except me.

—So lighten up—don't get serious about this! It's only a test.

I'll never forget what one of my greatest teachers from the 1970s told me: *There is no such thing as a stressful situation. There is only a stressful reaction.* Think about it: Two salespeople encounter the same prospect. One is intimidated, over-whelmed, paralyzed. The other handles the prospect with skill and proceeds to do business. The first reacts, the second responds. Stressful reactions come from your Child. Skillful responses come from your Adult. You have a choice. And so do your salespeople.

Exercise

1. Give your sales staff an understanding of the Parent, Adult and Child ego states, as well as OK/not—OK positions.

2. You play the role of prospect/client, presenting them with challenging questions and statements. You should ask the same question from three different ego states—Critical Parent, Adult, and Child.

3. After each comment you make, the group (or individuals you've selected from the group) identifies which ego state was speaking, and how they feel as a result.

4. They will learn that the same information, complaint, objection, or question can be expressed differently, generating different feelings in them.

5. Ask your people what part of the encounter they can control, and what part is beyond their control. Your people will eventually realize that they only piece they can control is how they react, how they feel, and how they respond.

6. Next, have them respond to your comments from step 2 with their Adapted Child. On purpose. They'll all laugh at how wimpy they sound, but this will be the laughter of self-recognition. They recognize their own responses from the past.

7. Have them practice responding to Critical Parent questions and comments from their Nurturing Parent and

their Adult.

Note: This exercise sets the stage for your coaching comments to come later, when you debrief sales calls and uncover wimpy behavior.

I'm often asked about how successfully some salespeople can control their Adapted Child. Are we fighting a losing battle here? The answer obviously depends on the person we're considering, but I've learned one strategy that works best with high need for approval. You don't have to eliminate this need. Instead, at first it's more practical to help the salesperson transfer it from the client to you. Rather than get approval from his prospects and clients,—usually by not asking tough questions, not asking for decisions and commitments, and not asserting himself—you will coach him to do these things in order to gain your approval. In addition, you will give him permission not to be perfect, even to fail at times.

As your salespeople grow more independent and less needy, they will naturally wean themselves from your approval as well as their clients'. (More about this in the next chapter.)

Chapter 3

Managing to Change

There's No Growth Without Change

It's only the Adult ego state that's capable of learning new things and integrating them into the entire personality. Consequently, if we're going to be successful in helping someone like Karen from the last chapter to change and grow, we'll need to have an Adult-to-Adult conversation. Here's a formula that's proved effective over the years:

1. Awareness of problem

2. Admission of problem

3. Cost of problem

4. Commitment to change results (get rid of problem)

5. Collaborative action

6. Track change

7. Regular updates

8. Rewards

Notice that I didn't say "foolproof" or "guaranteed." That is because you cannot force anyone to change—or to grow. I've used this formula with hundreds of salespeople over the years. Twenty-five percent of the people resisted strongly at some point, and we saw little change or growth. If you're willing to accept a 75 percent success rate, please read on.

We're assuming here that as a manager you have enough authority in your organization to employ the following eight steps.

1. Awareness of the problem. Amazingly, some salespeople don't see the problem. They may blame their customers, your pricing, the business or sales cycle, or even you for their own shortcomings. They may not see anything wrong with their performance. What's more likely is that they may not want...

2. To admit to you, or to themselves where they're falling short. This can start with comments like, "It really isn't that bad. I'm doing OK. There are other salespeople who rank below me." You can get them to move beyond this step when you have an objective discussion about...

3. The cost of their behavior. How it's affecting them, their income, their career, the team, the company, even their clients and prospects. This step is essential if you're going to be able to move forward and get a...

4. Commitment to change. We know if you do what you've always done, you'll get what you've always got, assuming the competition doesn't catch up and pass you by. It's the Child inside us that wants better results without having to work for them. She can't do it by herself. If she could, she would have already done so. Consequently...

5. You will suggest specific strategies and actions that Karen can take, and get a commitment from her to adopt

certain ones. She must also accept that…

6. You will be monitoring and tracking her results, and that…

7. You'll both be meeting to discuss the ups and downs of this process as it unfolds. Finally, you will…

8. Establish appropriate rewards for growth along the way. In TA terms this is called "feeding" or "rewarding" your Child (which doesn't want to do this work anyway).

Which step is most important to guarantee success? Although you can't really skip any of them, nothing will happen without Karen's commitment to change. You can't force or demand commitment. From your Critical Parent you can threaten her until she agrees to make changes, but we all know (including Karen) that threats rarely generate real commitments from anybody. Reasoning (from your Adult) with her while being sensitive (your Nurturing Parent) to her not—OK feelings leads to a successful change in behavior.

Before we see how this eight-step process might play out, consider what I call the Rules of Engagement:

1. Keep the conversation Adult to Adult.

2. If she starts to get defensive or to make excuses, she's in her Child. Stop the process and help her get back into her Adult.

3. If she notices that you are coming from your Critical Parent, she should stop the process and help you get back into your Adult.

Use your Nurturing Parent to help her through the difficult parts of the process.

The following conversation actually took place 20 years ago. I know, because I was the manager.

You: Karen, I wanted to have this meeting with you to discuss some things I've been noticing for a while. I'd like to find out if you're seeing them the same way.

Karen: What do you mean?

You: Well, for one, I track each salesperson and how often they come to me to ask for customer discounts. Naturally, I also track the average gross profit of each salesperson. I also notice things like the length of the sales cycle, how much time salespeople spend helping and servicing clients after the sale, and believe it or not, how much fun I think they're having.

Karen: That's a lot of tracking.

You: Yes, it is. And I want to discuss with you some of what I've observed. First of all, how would you rate yourself on asking for discounts for your customers? Do you see that as a strength or a weakness on your part?

Karen: Well, I guess it's not exactly a strength, but for us to be competitive, we have to discount sometimes.

You: Perhaps. Based on what I've seen, right now I'd have to say this is not one of your strengths—we can call it a weakness. I want to talk a little bit about where that's heading and about how it's affecting you. Obviously, you've computed that based on your commissions, it's not costing you much when you give a discount one time, right? Let's consider what happens afterwards with that client. What expectation are we establishing?

Karen: I guess he's likely to expect discounts again.

You: And how many orders do you expect to get from a typical client in a year's time? I think we covered that at our last sales meeting.

Karen: I think you said an average of five to six a year.

You: Let's do the math. Five to six discounts of 15 percent over a year, assuming the size of their orders stays about the same, is equivalent to a one-time discount every year of 75 to 90 percent, right? Now even if you're prepared to give away that much every year, we have to consider whether the company is also prepared to do the same with its share, right?

Karen: I guess so.

You: Let's look at a couple of other things, such as how this affects your future ability to take control of that client relationship. And even more important, what this is doing to your ability to control other clients and their expectations? I'm sure you understand that allowing one client to convince you he needs a discount makes it easier for you to hear and believe that from customers as well. In fact, I would have to say that this is what's been happening to some extent with you. Would you agree?

Karen: Well, I don't come to you all the time about this, but with certain customers we're just not going to get their business if we aren't more competitive with our pricing.

You: Karen, when you discount, it leads to very specific and predictable outcomes. Would you agree that one outcome is less money for you and us?

Karen: Sure.

You: A second outcome is that the client—whether justified or not—will expect future discounts. Do you agree?

Karen: Yes.

You: A third outcome is perhaps the most important one: it changes your expectations about what you're going to have to do to get and keep business. Do you see that?

Karen: Well, maybe. But every client is different, and every situation is different.

You: Karen, it's important that you step back and see the pattern or trend here. You have excellent analytical skills. You're right: Every situation is different. And you know your expectations and beliefs can either help you or hurt you in any situation, because they strengthen or weaken you as a negotiator, don't they?

Karen: I guess so.

You: For instance, if you really believed that every client needed a

15 percent discount for us to become one of their suppliers, wouldn't that belief determine your expectation about what was going to happen on a specific sales call? And wouldn't it have an overall weakening effect on your sales ability?

Karen: Sure, but I don't think that.

You: I know you don't. Let's take it a step further. If you did have that belief, wouldn't it keep you from earning the kind of money you need to make?

Karen: Yes.

You: And what would that do to your career?

Karen: I understand where we're going.

You: Karen, one additional thing I'd like you to consider. And that's how this entire process affects how you see yourself. What is this doing to your self-confidence?

Karen: You're making this sound like a total disaster! I don't really think every client needs a discount. There are just certain accounts where we need to be a little more flexible with our pricing.

You: Can we agree that to the extent you *do* think along these lines, and with the frequency you believe this, all these consequences will occur?

Karen: I guess so.

You: Karen, are you ready to do what's necessary to make sure these things *don't* happen? Are you ready to start making more money—for you and for us—with every order? And ready to gain more confidence in abilities, which are already considerable?

Karen: What will I have to do?

You: Karen, I think I'm hearing that you aren't sure you can do this. Is that a fair assessment?

Karen: Well, it does depend somewhat on what you're asking me to do here.

You: OK, let's figure this out together. We're going to need to talk about your expectations. What you think will happen on each selling appointment. Yes?

Karen: Yes, I can see how that would help.

You: And we're going to have to make sure that you are saying what needs to be said, especially when you hear those price objections and threats about giving the order to the competition. Right?

Karen: OK. That makes sense.

You: Actually, there's another important item we haven't brought up yet—at least in this conversation.

Karen: What's that?

You: Remember in past sales meetings when we discussed how need for approval can handicap you at every step along the way in doing business?

Karen: Yes, I remember.

You: I remember you telling me that this might be a problem for you. Wanting everyone to really like you and approve of your actions?

Karen: Yes, but everybody wants to be liked.

You: You're right, Karen. We all want to be liked. The real issue here is how much we *need* to be liked. After all, it's not *wanting* approval but need for approval that's the problem. Can you see how your *need* for approval might have a lot to do with this frequent discounting problem?

Karen: I'm sure it plays some part in it.

You: I agree. And unless we deal with this part of it, we're not going to be as successful with the rest of it. Are you willing to work with me on lowering your need for approval, especially from some of your key accounts?

Karen: I think so.

You: Karen, as you lower your need for approval, can you see that helping you not only with your accounts, but with the staff here in the office and even in your personal life?

Karen: Sure, I can see some benefits there too.

You: Let's talk specifically how we're going to proceed. But I'm going to need you to trust me—to trust that I'm doing this, working with you, so you can get better, be stronger, be more successful, and even enjoy what you're doing more. Are we on the same page here?

Karen: Sure. I trust you.

You: Thanks. And you want all these outcomes I just mentioned, yes?

Karen: I do. I want to be more successful. And I definitely want to enjoy selling and my interactions with clients more than I do now. I want to get better at all of it..

You: Great. Then starting with trust, I'm going to ask you to tell me how you're feeling before you go on some of these key account calls, especially the ones where you know they might be fighting us on price. And we're going to spend some time preparing you, helping you "get your head on straight" about what's going to happen. OK?

Karen: Yes. I'm OK with that.

You: In addition to preparing for these calls, we're going to spend some time debriefing afterward, to make sure that we're on track, or to get back on track, with what we're thinking, what we're saying, how we're reacting. OK?

Karen: Yes. That would be helpful. It sounds like this is going to take a lot of time.

You: I'm willing to make that investment in you, because I know you're worth it. But let me add that you have to do your part. You have to be open and honest with me, and if you tell me you're going to say or ask a client something, you'll actually do it. Fair enough?

Karen: OK, I'll do that. How often will we be meeting?

You: That depends on which accounts you're seeing, and how you're feeling about them and yourself. Initially, I'd say we're going to be meeting three times a week, 30 to 45 minutes each meeting—some in preparation, some in debriefing. Are you willing to make that investment to get better results?

Karen: Sure, I'm willing.

You: Good. So will I. It's a partnership—as long as we both put in 50 percent, it's a win-win situation, and we're both going to be happy with the results. Does that make sense?

Karen: Yes!

You: I'm sure you realize the road ahead of us won't be totally smooth. There will be bumps along the way. I want you to feel good about what we're doing together, even when it becomes difficult. Let's talk about how you're going to reward yourself along the way.

Karen: What do you mean?

You: Well, I know you love horses, and that you ride whenever you can. I've been thinking about this, and I suggest we structure a riding afternoon, perhaps on a Friday, that you're going to be earning as you make progress. How does that sound?

Karen: Hey, that would be great!

You: I thought you'd like it. Now this will be something you really earn, from stretching outside your comfort zone, along with my help. It's not going to come without some hard work. Understand?

Karen: I know it. But as long as I'm going to be doing this stuff and growing, I might as well get the rewards too.

You: I couldn't agree more. I'll work up some milestones I'd like to see you hit in the coming weeks, and the next time we meet, we'll consider them and agree on a timetable.

Karen: I'm looking forward to it.

You: Fine. So why don't we start by looking at the appointments you have set up for the next three days....

This one conversation obviously won't eliminate or even reduce Karen's need for approval. What it has done is brought this to her conscious awareness so she can recognize it in the future and be better prepared. Karen's need for approval won't disappear quickly. Initially, she's more likely to transfer it from her customers to you, her manager. But wouldn't you rather your salespeople need your approval than the approval of their clients and prospects? Having them seek and get their love from you instead of from those people they're trying to sell is a good start to growing profitable sales. We switched the last few steps around, because that's how the conversation unfolded. The sequence isn't as important as covering all the points.

The reward—in this case the riding day—should be customized to fit your salesperson. Here's another example: Alan, a brilliant consultant for a software firm, was a master at solving client problems. His challenge was a paralyzing fear of cold calls, or talking to anybody he didn't know. This even included incoming voicemail messages, asking for a return call! Alan certainly had the don't-talk-to-strangers message carved in stone in his Child ego state.

The building where Alan worked was in a beautiful office park, with a lake and woods and delightful walking paths. Alan loved to take walks there, and he did this when he should have been making phone calls to set appointments.

Understanding all behavior as having a positive intent (thanks to Bill, the neuropsychologist, remember?), his manager Anna could always tell when Alan was avoiding those parts of his job that made him uncomfortable. She would look out her window, see Alan walking down the path by the lake, and start fuming. She often criticized his avoidance behavior when he returned. She spoke from her Critical Parent, and Alan, receiving this message in his Child, felt dutifully guilty. In his Adult he knew Anna was right, and his own Parent told him he should be doing his work. He even admitted that his own Parent ego state was more critical of his behavior than Anna was. (Occasionally a salesperson is more critical of himself than is his manager.)

When I saw what was happening, it was easy to identify the solution. Here's what we did: After Alan had made five phone calls—that's contacts or conversations—he had earned a walk in the woods. Now he could really enjoy his walk, guilt-free. And Anna would feel good whenever she saw Alan walking outside. Rewards don't have to be expensive to be effective.

Right about now you may be saying to yourself:

1. Wow, there's a lot to this Managing the Child inside my people.

2. I'm not sure I want to make this kind of investment, especially the time investment. After all, this salesperson is already taking up lots of my time.

3. I'm not sure I'm up to this.

Let me respond:

1. Yes, there is a lot to it. But once you learn the process, it becomes more natural, less complicated, and even fun. It's kind of like when you first learned to ride a bike: impossibly difficult the first time, easier the second day, and by the third or fourth day, you can't remember what was so challenging.

2. Guess what—you're already making the investment! You've been paying Karen her base salary and benefits, in spite of the fact that she hasn't been as productive as you need her to be. You've been spending time with her–and even more time thinking about her and her problems—but until now that hasn't helped much. You're going to be

working smarter, and probably a little harder, but that's what effective management is about, at least when you're implementing new strategies. The time you spend with her will be focused on her making changes, instead of on her rationales, excuses, and digressions.

3. If you're having doubts at this point, it's not unusual. The following points will help:

❖ You're new at this, as is Karen. Neither of you has to be perfect in order to "get it right." As you both put your attention on the real issues, she will get stronger.

❖ As you spend more time with these strategies, you'll get better.

❖ Remember: If you want a new crop, you have to plant a new seed. You can't expect to get different results by doing the same things you've been doing-and neither can Karen.

❖ This is on-the-job-training for both of you, although Karen won't realize this.

It's helpful to view this process as an adventure in learning how to grow people. Actually, that's not a bad way to view your job—especially if you want to enjoy it.

Are These People Keepers"?

I'm often asked if there's really a place in sales for people with a very strong Adapted Child ego state. The answer is not a simple one. Certainly they might find it easier in a sales service role, where keeping the client happy is a primary focus. High Adapted Child people, if they are committed enough to their own development for their own reasons, can grow out of this. It takes time and coaching on your part—and a lot of work on theirs.

Back in the 1980s I received a call from Anita, who had

been referred to me by a client. She had recently retired from the Internal Revenue Service (IRS) where she worked as an auditor. Now she was trying to start a consulting business helping small businesses avoid IRS audits. She obviously had valuable knowledge, but she lacked selling skills. Even more important, her Adapted Child was too strong, manifesting in need for approval and fear of rejection. After coaching her for some time, it was clear that unless she could get control of her Adapted Child, she wasn't going to grow her practice successfully. Back in those days I held a twice-monthly training meeting for my local clients. They came to discuss their selling problems, and I served as both sales manager and coach. Anita would attend regularly, and this time, there were about 30 people in the room from different companies and industries. She offered up a selling problem, which stemmed from her Adapted Child. This time, instead of offering advice, I asked her if she was ready to deal with the real issue. After some explanation to the entire group about how emotions and fears undermine our efforts, Anita said she was ready to meet her challenge. I told her we could go through an exercise that would eliminate some of her fears, but that it wouldn't be much fun. After she again gave me permission to move forward. Here's what we did.

Anita came to the front of the room and faced the rest of the group. Each person in turn came up to her and told her "No!" to her face. Some said it roughly, some spoke with tact, but everyone was clear about their message. With some responses she smiled, and with others she obviously felt rejected and hurt. The exercise took about 10 minutes. When everybody had taken a shot at her, she looked at me. The first words out of her mouth were, "I'm still standing!" Then she grinned. The grin became wider until she laughed, her eyes glowing. Everyone stood and applauded for Anita. She was the first to say that it would never be this tough for her in front of a prospect, and everyone in the room agreed.

We then focused on what to ask after her prospect said, "No." As with most salespeople, Anita's fears were far worse than the actual event, and her prospects were always polite with her. She learned how to ask, from her Nurturing Parent, why they didn't want her help and what the real issue was. In the weeks that followed, Anita's confidence improved along with her sales techniques. Although she still found herself in her Child from time to time, she no longer stayed stuck there. She eventually developed a profitable consulting practice and grew to enjoy selling. Anita was a classic example of success in sales resulting from learning to get her Adapted Child under control.

Chapter 4

Managing Your Other "Children"

Kindergarten Cop

Let's turn our attention now to the Natural Child and the Rebellious Child (also called Little Professor). They pose their own unique challenges.

The Natural Child

He's looking for a good time—now. He may have a short attention span—A.D.D., anyone? Let's take Jeremy as an example. He gets along well with customers who are like-minded, but may be discounted by more serious, businesslike prospects. He's occasionally makes inappropriate remarks or jokes at odd times. Impulse control is not his strength, and this can cost him (and his company) when he says the wrong thing at the wrong time to a customer. He's typically enthusiastic about things he enjoys, loves excitement, and can be productive when he gets on a roll. His momentum can fade suddenly, and then his production falls off. Most young children have yet to develop a long-term view, and neither has Jeremy. There could be several reasons, but the bottom line is that he hasn't grown up yet.

If you manage a Jeremy, you experience periodic frustration with him, after which you probably give him motivational pep talks or read him the riot act, finally leaving him alone for a while. Nobody, including the rest of your sales staff, is going to depend on him for too much. So what else can you do, aside from lowering your expectations? How can you help him "grow up"?

I've found that the same eight-step process we discussed two chapters ago is your strategy. But a warning here: Just as you must give younger, less mature children more frequent reminders, praise, and rewards, you'll need to adopt the same strategy with these Natural Children. They generally are aware of their shortcomings and will often admit to them. But you can help them grow over time, but you'll need both patience and creativity with them; patience for when they backslide, and creativity in coming up with new rewards that keep them engaged.

Here again are the eight steps you'll want to employ:

1. Awareness of problem

2. Admission of problem

3. Cost of problem

4. Commitment to change results (get rid of problem)

5. Collaborative action

6. Track change

7. Regular updates

8. Rewards

At a financial services firm in the 1990s, Claire was moderately successful financial advisor who should have been doing much better. Her manager told me that she'd hit periods of little production, and then have a great burst of activity that brought in several new clients, mostly from cold calling. After sitting with her and her manager to discuss her pattern of behavior and results, she decided it was time for a change. Claire had two reasons for wanting this. First, she wanted to move out of her apartment and buy a house, and she needed an extra $25,000 in six months for a down payment. Her second reason was even better: For years her older siblings had always teased her about being the tagalong baby sister, always following their lead. This still bothered her, and she wanted to show them she could be successful on her own.

We explained to her that she would need to take a more long-term view of her business than she was used to doing. We put together a program of daily and weekly activities, along with Tuesday and Friday meetings with her manager. She called me on Monday mornings to review the previous week's sales calls, and I offered encouragement and suggestions about strategy and technique.

We knew that this plan and activity would fail unless we could keep her involved and motivated, and for that we needed her attention. Claire was a real audiophile with an expensive stereo system, who loved adding to her CD collection. So we established a contract with her whereby every day that she hit her quota of conversations with potential clients—through cold calls, networking, chance encounters, referrals—she would buy herself another CD. She was excited about this, and my Monday morning meetings with her always began with, "How many CDs did you buy last week?"

For this kind of sales management program to work, the Child has to be able to receive rewards along the way.

The Rebellious Child (The Little Professor)

He's creative, manipulative, intuitive, looking for short-cuts, continuously bending the rules to his advantage, and not above stretching the truth when necessary—and he'll be the one to decide when it's necessary. His strengths: He's creative, manipulative, intuitive, looking for shortcuts—you get the picture. The downside: he's difficult to manage because you can't be sure when he's "working you" and not just the client. He's the one on your team who sometimes goes "too far," and when he gets caught, you find yourself intervening to save his accounts.

This personality can be the most challenging to manage. You may find yourself working to stay one step ahead of him in the management process. He can sometimes bring in the big sale and salvage an account that looks lost. But he may not generate much trust from other salespeople, from you, and worst of all, from his accounts.

We hired Tony as a sales rep for a client who sold computer peripherals. Tony scored higher on the Little Professor scale than anyone I had ever seen. He also had a pretty good track record and was fearless. It was an interesting combination, and we decided to take a chance on him. I told the manager to monitor him closely, including a daily debriefing at 5 p.m. During the first three months, Tony brought in some good business, and he exceeded his quota. He also missed five days of work during that period because of "illness" and "personal family reasons." The daily debriefs actually took place only about twice a week, because Tony was usually "on the other side of town" or with clients, and couldn't make it back in time.

One day I was scheduled to conduct a sales training session, and I arrived early. At 2:45 p.m., 15 minutes before the meeting, a middle-aged man came to the front office looking for Tony. The receptionist said he hadn't arrived yet but was due in shortly. Saying he'd catch up with Tony later, the man left. Tony showed up at 3:10 for our meeting, apologizing for being late. At 4:30, when the training ended, he walked out to the parking lot and returned a minute later. Sheepishly, he asked if somebody could give him a lift home. When we asked him what was going on, he admitted that his car had been repossessed. He had missed too many payments. We had to decide that Tony was working too many angles to keep him on board, in spite of his sales ability, and we gave him cab fare, along with severance pay.

This was an extreme case, but it demonstrates the difficulty in taming the manipulator inside people. Instead of Tony, you're more likely to have salespeople who bend the rules a little too far to get what they want. It's important that you set strict boundaries of acceptable behavior and penalties for breaking the rules with these individuals.

On the positive side, I've found that the Little Professor is eager to accept and try new sales techniques. He recognizes when clients and prospects are manipulating him. His view of the selling world is more realistic (even cynical) and less idealistic, so he's not as vulnerable to being misled or manipulated. Where other salespeople may be too trusting of prospects, he takes everything with several grains of salt. He'll question the validity of statements and claims that prospects make. And—in moderation—isn't that an important quality you want in your salespeople?

Getting better results from salespeople with a strong Little Professor can be an ongoing challenge. Start with the eight-step process, and you'll probably have to spend more time on the steps 2 and 3. People like Tony won't readily admit to the problem, and they can come up with many reasons or rationalizations why it's not costing them much. The key here is to let them know you are aware of what they are doing, and that whenever you see potential harm you'll step in. Get a commitment from them that they won't allow things to get to the point where damage control is required. Their growth comes as they learn how to recognize appropriate boundaries in their behavior.

I've used one additional approach with them that works well and is even enjoyable. I say, *I'll accept any rationale or explanation you give me for your actions, but only if it meets the following condition: It must be new to me. If I've heard it before, it won't wash.*

These Rebellious Children like having fun and working angles. I won't deny them that. Just don't bore me with a story I've heard before.

Where does all this leave us with the Natural Child and the Rebellious Child? It leaves us with people—sometimes immature, sometimes needy, and sometimes manipulative, all in varying degrees.

Clients invariably ask me, *Is there an ideal mixture? What's the balance we're trying to find or develop in our salespeople?*

The ideal mixture probably only exists in an ideal world. In our world we have to work with what we have. If your people are receptive to learning about themselves so they can get better results, we have real potential for growth. That said, you will find that many of your salespeople need to lower their need for approval, which stems from their Adapted Child. Some also need to strengthen their intuitive and manipulative abilities, which reside in their Rebellious Child. A few will need to learn to become more—or less—playful, at least on the job.

Below is a sample bar graph, an egogram in TA terms that

shows the ego state scores from one of my surveys. The egogram allows us to view a personality quickly and comprehensively. We will refer to the individual ego states by their initials—CP (Critical Parent), NP (Nurturing Parent), A (Adult), NC (Natural Child), LP (Little Professor, or Rebellious Child), and AC (Adapted Child).

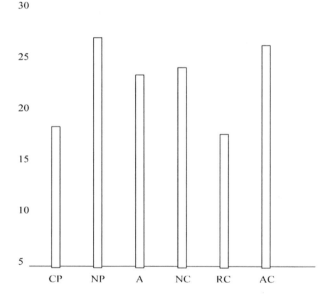

Notice the relatively high score for Adapted Child. This indicates that this salesperson has high need for approval and will be vulnerable to the corresponding selling situations we discussed earlier. Although not necessarily a "deal breaker," it's a definite warning signal. The high Adapted Child can be reduced, but as you saw in the last chapter, it takes time and effort.

When I survey the ego states of salespeople, I look for certain relationships. Nurturing Parent scores should be higher than Critical Parent scores; the salesperson must be capable of asking questions and negotiating without appearing aggressive. Higher CP scores (than NP) translate into coming across too strong when eliciting information or responding to concerns and objections. These salespeople often admit that they sometimes lose accounts due to their aggressiveness, and many are looking for a better sales approach.

What constitutes a "high score"? On the surveys I use, the absolute numbers aren't quite as significant as their relationships to one another, the relative scores. In this example, with a maximum score of 35, you can see that the individual has a high NP when compared to the CP, and when viewed by itself. Is this good? Well, we also have to consider the other ego states, especially the relationship between the Rebellious Child and the Adapted Child. Which score would you want to be higher in your salespeople? You'd want the AC score to be low in those people who have to prospect, to close, to negotiate, to stand their ground with tough clients. I often refer to the AC score as the "wimp factor." A strong RC doesn't hurt here either—manipulation can be a good thing when used properly.

Years ago I was working with a medical technology company, and in the training session where I introduced these concepts, all the employees were in attendance. Along with the sales staff and management, administrators and delivery people were there to learn as well. We discussed and interpreted different people's scores. As we broke for intermission, a woman named Ellen approached me and showed me some striking numbers. They were:

NP = 32

AC = 33

RC = 7

"What is your job here?" I asked.

"I'm in accounts receivable—collections," she replied.

I smiled and excused myself, heading straight for the company president. I took him aside and asked him how severe his cash flow problems were. He smiled sheepishly and asked, "How did you know?" I explained to him that he can't entrust his collection efforts to a personality with such high need for approval (AC) and who is incapable of manipulation (RC). She's negotiating with people who give her stalls and make excuses, and she probably will do anything to avoid confrontation and tension! He reassigned Ellen and replaced her with somebody who had a personality more suited for the job.

As a successful manager of people you must understand their fears and emotional needs, and help them outgrow them. As we'll see in the next chapter, you are in the growth business.

Chapter 5

The Growth Continuum

How Far Is Too Far?

In my workshops, I use the growth continuum graph below to explain to both salespeople and managers how we grow—and how we outgrow our Child.

Two vertical lines define the area within which 99 percent of all salespeople act. The left boundary (TW) stands for Total Wimp. The right (TF) stands for Too Far.

At or near the Total Wimp line, selling is a continuous not-OK experience. Salespeople selling from here are afraid to say anything that might potentially upset anyone. Fear of rocking the boat or of coming across too strong and losing are always in their awareness. Too Far is the line beyond which salespeople are overly aggressive and abrasive, blowing prospects out of the water and ruining relationships.

In TA terms, TW is the neighborhood ruled by the Adapted Child, acting as a governor for every thought and action. TF is territory the Adapted Child has heard about but never visited. In fact, many years ago their Adapted Child internalized the warning to avoid this threatening area at all costs.

It's my experience that we all have an internal psychological thermostat that constantly signals where we are at any given moment. And where we are most often is in our comfort zone. It feels safe and secure, because we've been there so often. When we're in challenging selling situations, the lights and volume on the thermostat are turned up several notches. I'm further convinced that for about 98 percent of us, our thermostat is broken, sending a false danger signal. We think—we feel—we're certain—that we're about to enter Too Far territory, when in actuality we may not even be close. And as a result, we repeatedly, habitually, maddeningly stop short for fear of going too far.

Some examples:

❖ You know that the client is feeding you a line, but don't call him on it.

❖ Your prospect just said, "Call me back in a couple of weeks, and I'll give you my answer." You know what you want to say, but think, *If I come back too hard, he'll be offended and I'll lose my chance.* So you reply, "I'll be glad to. How about Thursday?"

❖ Your client says that you're going to have to give him better pricing if you want to retain his business, and even though you know your price is both fair and competitive, you respond, "Let me work on it and I'll see what we can do."

❖ Your prospect tells you he's seen your competitor's presentations, and he's leaning toward going with them. Instead of asking where your competitor's strengths and weaknesses lie, you hear yourself offering to throw in a one-year maintenance contract to win his favor.

As a manager, your objective is much the same as mine: Moving your people from the left side of that line to the right side, away from TW and toward TF, on a daily basis. We want our salespeople to feel comfortable (OK) operating in the space that is just short of Too Far. This of course is where you find your top producers. Selling from here means having more control—control of themselves, control of their clients and control of what happens between them. And this of course translates into:

1. More money

2. More enjoyment from selling

Around 1990 I was doing a workshop for a client—RJO, a high-tech company marketing to the federal government. As I was explaining this growth process, Chief Executive Officer Dick Otero interrupted me. He walked up to the screen where the growth continuum was displayed, put his hand on the Too Far line, and said, "I'll give $1,000 to anyone here who crosses this line!"

Dick was aware that his business development people had no idea where that line was, but he was trying to push them toward it. He himself had become extremely successful—and wealthy—by doing business from the point just short of Too Far.

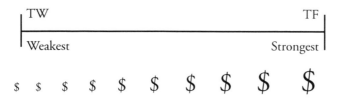

We have a technical term for this movement from left to right. It's called *growth*!

Exercise

List three healthy activities you're currently engaged in that five to seven years ago, if you had considered them, you would have said, "No way!" They could include things such as managing a large sales force, scuba diving with sharks, breaking 85 on the golf course, being married to the partner of your dreams, running a marathon, or no longer smoking. You get the picture. So you've grown in the past several years. Have you made the decision to stop growing? Of course not!

1.

2.

3.

Managing Growth

Let's return to the growth continuum. My point is simple: What seems like Too Far today can become quite comfortable and natural tomorrow. This is what growth is all about. It's a mistake to allow our beliefs to limit our development. Just because a bar seems too high to hurdle today, this doesn't mean we can't jump it tomorrow. I advise managers to keep a growth continuum chart on each of their salespeople. Have regular discussions with them about where they are and how they're going to move from left to right. Any quarterly or annual reviews you conduct should take their growth into consideration.

Managers often find that they get the greatest return on their investment of time and energy by focusing on those salespeople who haven't yet reached the top. They may only be half way to the largest dollar sign on the growth continuum. As long as they have a passion to be successful and are willing to confront their fears, it makes sense to invest in them.

If You Sell

1. Keep your own chart. Be honest about where you think you are, and in which areas you need to move toward the Too Far line in order to become more successful.

2. You can rate yourself in categories such as:

—Maintaining your poise when a prospect throws you a tough question or objection

—Comfortably addressing issues where your company is at a disadvantage

—Asking your client where you stand compared with

the competition

—Addressing issues where your client is misinformed about your capabilities versus the competition

3. Show your chart with your manager. Have a candid discussion. What messages do you think that would send to your manager about how committed you are to your success? The discussion may provide you with insight about how your manager sees you, which could be different than how you view yourself.

4. In addition to working on your business, you need to work on yourself. As you eliminate your own weaknesses by stretching outside your comfort zone, you'll be delighted at how much easier and more profitable selling becomes.

As a manager you know that there can be no growth without change. Every step forward into uncharted territory is a step farther away from what's familiar. And this can feel unsafe—the ultimate not-OK feeling. If you've seen a child being dragged into a dentist's office, you've got the image of what many salespeople experience when faced with change. Managers often take on the parental role when asking or demanding that others change. If you don't address the fears that underlie most resistance to change, it's unlikely that you'll see much growth. It's ultimately the Nurturing Parent inside the salesperson that tells his Child, "You'll be OK. We have to do this." You'll want to let your salesperson know that he'll have your support and encouragement as he moves out of his comfort zone and into the unknown. He knows that he should (Parent) do it. You'll teach him how (Adult) to do it. You may need to remind him that success never comes when your Child is in control.

It's been said of life's winners that their desire for success is greater than their fear of failure. This doesn't mean successful people are without fear. They face their fears with intelligent action; we call this courage. As you help your salespeople grow, their comfort zone gets bigger and the options available to them in every selling situation increase. This translates into greater control and better results. It's all about growth, and your salespeople should understand that they're in the growth business just as you are.

Exercise

Here's an exercise your salespeople will learn from and enjoy.

1. Draw the growth continuum on the board.

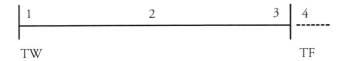

2. You give the group objections, stalls, challenges, and irrational statements, just like a prospect on a sales call. They can include:

❖ ABC Co. said their technology far outpaces yours.

❖ ABC Co.(your competitor) said with your services we're paying for whistles and bells we don't really need.

❖ ABC Co. said they would throw in free maintenance for two years if we sign with them.

❖ All the solutions we've they've seen are pretty much the same. It doesn't make sense for us them to spend extra dollars on whistles and bells we don't need.

❖ If you want our business, you need to be more competitive.

❖ We have decided to put the decision on the backburner for now.

❖ Why don't you just send me a proposal, and I'll get back to you.

❖ We've been quite impressed with the proposal that ABC Co. gave us.

Have the group come up with three to four responses for each one, as follows:

—Their first response (from position #1) must be from territory closest to TW. (These will be most familiar to them.)

—The next response (2) should be from a point half way between TW and TF. This will be an improvement, but still not the best.

—The third response (3) is the strongest reply without going too far.

—The group can even offer a response from a point past the TF line (4). They'll really enjoy this one.

3. The group discusses which response they're most comfortable with and why, and then which one will be most effective and why.

4. At the end of the exercise, each person commits to use one of the responses that's outside his comfort zone and which represents growth for him.

How will this exercise help strengthen your staff? First, many of them will realize for the first time how far they have to go before they go too far. Second, these same people will learn how and why to use stronger responses to objections and statements they hear every day. Third, they'll have the experience of stretching outside their comfort zone in a safe setting. Importantly, you will have the opportunity to observe how they handle all this. You'll find that this exercise generates enthusiastic participation and produces results.

Chapter 6

Eliminating Excuses

Yes...But; I'm trying; It's Not My fault!

Successful people don't make excuses; they have no reason to do so. But excuses will prevent growth. They poison potential success. Excuse-making can even destroy careers. You can count on excuses generating more trouble than you can handle, including:

For managers:

❖ Exasperation with salespeople who don't improve

❖ Frustration with selling situations that don't get resolved

❖ Inaccurate forecasting

❖ Failure to hit revenue and profit targets

❖ Not knowing what you can count on from some of your staff

❖ Knowing you can't count on some of your staff

❖ Poor morale

❖ Anger directed at the salespeople giving you the excuses, instead of taking responsibility for your part in this process

Remember Bill from the introduction? Here's where we going to help him address his problems, which include:

❖ Not getting any better at orchestrating client relationships

❖ Falling into a Childlike role with managers as he regularly offers reasons why his forecasts are off.

❖ Selling himself on why his income isn't growing.

❖ Blaming his clients whenever he buys their excuses.

❖ Feeling guilty for not doing the job he's paid to do.

❖ Not growing, personally or professionally.

Below, you can see the sequence of events that occurs repeatedly.

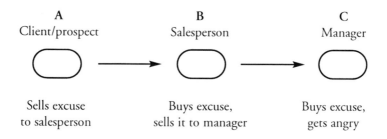

A	**B**	**C**
Client/prospect	Salesperson	Manager
Sells excuse to salesperson	Buys excuse, sells it to manager	Buys excuse, gets angry

Many salespeople find it easier to buy the excuses that clients give them (A), and then turn around and sell them (B) to their manager. If you in turn buy (C) the excuse, congratulations! You've helped create the perfect feedback loop to inhibit growth—the growth of your salesperson, the growth of your revenues and profits, and the growth of your own career.

Some key questions for you:

1. Does the salesperson recognize that the client's remarks are an excuse?

2. Is he aware that he's selling you the manager an excuse?

3. Are you aware that you're buying an excuse?

4. How will buying excuses affect your future?

Awareness is always the first step in fixing any problem. If you don't see where the problem starts, you're left fuming about symptoms and fallout. Excuses can become a cancer on any sales organization, and I've seen them destroy more than one sales force over years.

Here are some questions you can ask your salespeople to heighten their awareness of what may be happening.

1. Does he recognize what's happening?

❖ Bill, did you believe the client when he told you their budget was shot for this year?

❖ Was there any point in the conversation when you questioned his sincerity about this subject?

❖ What do you think would have happened if he had really wanted our solution? Would he have been able to find the money?

❖ How did you feel when the client told you about his budget? Did you feel even a little bit relieved—relieved that you didn't have to go up against him any longer this year?

❖ Let's assume for a minute that the client was giving you an excuse, hiding the real reason he didn't want to buy. How do you think he saw you when you accepted his explanation? How does he see you now?

❖ What do you think this has done for your ability to manage this client relationship, from now on?

❖ What have you learned from our conversation so far?

2. Does he realize he's trying to get you to buy the excuse?

❖ Bill, if I accept this explanation from you, aren't I allowing you to sell me this story, just as the client sold it to you?

❖ How does that serve you, me and our company?

❖ Bill, my job is to help you see what's really happening when you're out there selling, so that you can get to where you want to go and reach your goals. Do you agree?

❖ Do you see that if you're able to sell me on the client's excuse, then I'm actually keeping you from reaching your goals?

❖ Do you still want me to buy that story from you?

3 and 4. Am I aware that I'm "buying" and undermining my future?

❖ What would happen if I refused to accept Bill's explanation?

❖ What actions would Bill and I have to take next?

❖ Would these actions stand a better chance of us winning business?

❖ How will accepting Bill's explanation help us reach our goals with this account?

❖ Which strategic thinking and behavior patterns do I want to reinforce here?

❖ How long will top management accept these sub par results from me, and from my team?

❖ What is this doing to my career?

Note that almost all excuse-making comes from the Child ego state, specifically the Little Professor. The questions I asked above are directed to the Adult ego state. If you want to stop the excuse-making, your salesperson must be in his Adult ego state to understand and appreciate the process. All growth takes place in the Adult. As long as Bill is in his

Child, he cannot grow.

Parenting Lessons

When my son Jesse was about six years old, I had just told him for the umpteenth time that he had to make up his bed. He must not have been in the mood to hear another lecture from his father, so he did what six-year-old kids do—he covered his ears! Jesse was not ready (i.e., in his Adult) to learn or grow from my "expert" parental advice. And because I never sat at the head of the parenting class, my next move was to speak even louder and tell him again. You can imagine how effective that was. I don't actually remember if he got too old for me to lecture him about his room, or if I finally realized that what I was doing wasn't working. Anyway, we arrived at a workable solution when he went away to college. I stopped thinking about it; his room became his girlfriend's challenge.

Much of what I (and you) have learned from parenting is applicable to the world of sales management. Knowing how and when to pick your battles is a great lesson that applies to both. I recall telling Jesse when he was five or six years old that it was time to come home from a friend's house. He resisted because he was having such a good time. After a couple of exchanges, I asked, "Jesse, are you going to come quietly, or do I have to use earplugs?" You have to learn the difference between what you can control, and what you can't.

Since excuse-making comes from the Child ego state, our questions need to stimulate Bill to consider, analyze, digest, and evaluate what we're saying and formulate responses. In other words, we direct our conversation to Bill's Adult ego state.

When Bill doesn't take responsibility for his outcomes, he'll make an excuse. He looks outside himself, blaming the prospect, the economy, the budget, the weather, the planets—it really doesn't matter what he chooses. One excuse is as good—or as bad—as another.

When you hear excuses the most important thing you can do is to stop accepting them. Sounds insultingly simple, doesn't it? This action will produce powerful results. If you won't allow Bill to sell you excuses from his clients, he has only a few options:

1. He can stop buying them from his clients, which means he will have to figure out a better response when he hears them.

2. He can persist in trying to sell them to you and fail.

3. Eventually he will leave for another company where he hopes his new manager will buy the excuses he's selling.

Ultimately, any of these responses brings you an acceptable outcome. If you're going to stop accepting excuses you have to discuss your plan with Bill. Here's how the conversation might play out:

You: Bill, we've spoken before about what I believe are excuses that your clients are giving you, and that you're trying to get me to accept.

Bill: I know, but I really don't think they are excuses. These are real situations that don't go away.

You: I understand that you might think so, but unfortunately I don't. Can we agree on one key thing here?

Bill: What's that?

You: Bill, as long as you accept these excuses or explanations, you're not growing your business in these accounts. Is that true?

Bill: Well, I guess that's one way to look at it.

You: We need to see it that way, Bill, because that's reality for you. Your sales won't grow by accepting these excuses from your clients.

Bill: So what am I supposed to do?

You: Bill, that's the right question to ask. What do you need to do differently to get a different result?

Bill: I'm not sure. Maybe if I called on the client earlier before his budget was spent....

You: No, Bill, that won't work. If he's giving you an excuse, he can always give it to you when you call on him earlier. What do you need to do differently when you hear that from your client?

Bill: Maybe if I could convince them of the overall value we offer, that would help. You're always talking to us about that.

You: Yes, I continuously bring that up. But it sounds like you're not convinced of our value, and if you aren't, how are you going to convince anyone else?

Bill: I'm convinced. I know that we provide plenty of benefits that nobody else does. It's just that....

You: Bill, I have to interrupt you here. What I just heard from you didn't really convince me. Let me ask you—do you need to believe in what you sell?

Bill: Yes, definitely. But I believe in our products and how we back them up.

You: How effective are you at transferring that belief to your clients? Is that an area where, if you were stronger, it would help bring you better results?

Bill: I guess so.

You: Now we're getting somewhere. We can't stop the clients from saying what they're going to say. The only thing you can really control is how you respond. And you just told me that an important factor in what you say is what you believe.

Bill: Yes, that's right.

You: Can you stop clients from giving you excuses, Bill?

Bill: I don't see how I can do that.

You: I agree with you. You can only control how you feel, what you believe and what you say. Does that make sense?

Bill: Yes, it does.

You: Bill, if things are going to change, you're going to have to recognize when you're getting an excuse, and you're going to have to respond differently—if you want to get a different result. Right?

Bill: Yes.

You: There's really no other way, especially because I've made a decision about this. Here's what I've decided: Starting today, I will no longer accept anything from you that sounds like an excuse. Now why do you think I've made this decision?

Bill: I guess it's because you want more business from me.

You: That's certainly one reason. Can you think of any others?

Bill: Well, we do seem to spend a lot of time going back and forth on this stuff. And like you just said, I'm the one who is going to make a difference.

You: Good insight! We also need to consider that you're not showing enough progress. Your business isn't growing, and you're not growing as a person either. If I continue to accept excuses from you, because you accepted them from your clients, I'm actually inhibiting your growth. To the extent I've done that in the past, I'm truly sorry. But I'm not going to hurt you any more. You see, my job is to grow our business by helping our sales staff grow. And the most important way I can do that with you, is to stop accepting anything that sounds like an excuse. Got it?

Bill: Yes, but not everything I tell you is an excuse, you know.

You: Bill, that sounds like an excuse to me! You're better than that. If you're going to grow your business like we both want, this is going to be reason...I can't let you off the hook. Are you ready to hear what's going to happen?

Bill: OK.

You: From now on, when I hear something that sounds like an excuse, we're going to stop our discussion and deal with it. We'll be thinking this through, together—analyzing what happened on your sales call, how it happened, what you could have done to get a different result. Adult to Adult. In our discussions there will be no place for your Child ego state. I want you to grow and get stronger from every conversation we have, and this means no excuses. Do you understand why we're going down this path?

Bill: I think so.

You: Bill, I'd like you to consider for a moment what selling would be like for you if you no longer "bought" excuses from your clients…if you had an effective response for anything they threw at you…if you never dropped into your Child on a sales call. Does that sound appealing?

Bill: Yes, that would be great. But I think I'm a long way from that point.

You: Wherever you are, that's where we start. I'll do my part, but you must do yours. You have to be open and honest with me about what's happening on your sales calls—what they say and what you say. For now, that's all I'm asking. Are you willing to do that?

Bill: OK.

You: Bill, no excuses means taking responsibility for every outcome. As you go down this path, you have more control. As soon as you blame the client, his budget, his boss, you might as well blame the weather and the economy. One excuse is not much different than another. They're all barriers to your success.

Bill: What happens when there are situations I can't control?

You: We'll discuss what to do about them. You're going to find that it always begins with you, not with the situation, if you want control. If you control what you believe, say and do, the situations will work out fine, for the most part.

You: One other thing, Bill…you can't be perfect yet. You can't even be excellent. We're not there yet, so don't put that pressure on yourself. I certainly won't. OK? Just be who you are. That's good enough, because that's where we're starting. Do we have a deal?

Bill: Yes.

This isn't unlike the need for approval scenario in Chapter 3. In both cases we used the same formula to get the salesperson to address the problem and open up to change. In both cases we used our Nurturing Parent and our Adult to keep the salesperson in his/her Adult. In the real world of course discussions aren't neat and clean, and serious problems aren't resolved after five minutes. You also know that serious problems don't get resolved unless you both recognize and admit to them.

Another key part of this discussion is the partnership we developed with Bill. This is essential for moving forward. Think of how often you've tried to implement corrective action or programs without a partnership. If the other party hasn't bought into the problem, its severity or a corrective plan of action, there is no improvement. You can't manage successfully if your salespeople won't meet you halfway. That would be as futile continuing to lecture your child about making his bed when he's covered his ears with his hands. Who would be that foolish?

Are you an enabler in excuse-making? It should be clear by now that by "buying" excuses, you aren't helping; you're perpetuating the process. If you still can't determine if you are part of the problem, consider your sales staff as a group. If more than 25 percent of them are giving you excuses, guess what?—you are! So if two out of five, three out of ten, and so on are giving you excuses, you are giving them permission to do so and must work on yourself. Work harder on recognizing excuses and confronting your salespeople when you hear them.

What If They Resist?

They will.

You'll have to deal with it.

Let's discuss how.

It's the rare salesperson who thanks you as soon as you begin holding them more accountable for their actions, including accepting excuses from clients and prospects. You'll find that resistance to your changes lessens as you do the following:

1. Explain why you're doing what your doing

2. Explain who benefits (them, obviously) and how

3. Get them to see what their future might look like if they don't change and grow

A final note on excuses: I believe that winners take responsibility for everything that happens to them. As a matter of fact, that's one of the reasons they become winners. It's a description not just of the goal but also the path to continued success. If your salespeople will take responsibility for their outcomes, they're on the winning road. When's the last time you saw a successful individual looking for an excuse?

One of my favorite one-liners also happens to be the only sentence I know that's composed entirely of two-letter words: *If it is to be, it is up to me.*

I suggest distributing this sentence to your sales staff in advance of your next sales meeting. Write the sentence on a flipchart for everyone to see, and then open the discussion about what this means to their sales career. The only two rules are that everybody participates, and no critical comments are allowed. Reserve at least 30 minutes for an engaging and productive interaction. This exercise can be the start to helping some of your salespeople grow up and out of their Child ego state.

Chapter 7

Becoming an All-Star Coach

Hall of Fame Credentials

The world's top athletes, in every sport, have coaches. The reasons are always the same. They need:

❖ Somebody who can objectively evaluate their technique

❖ Somebody who can offer suggestions so they can improve

❖ Somebody who can suggest a regimen or program to ensure improvement

❖ Somebody who can tell them what they need to hear, even if they don't necessarily want to hear it

❖ Somebody who can give them a realistic idea of how effectively they can compete

❖ Somebody who can track their progress toward a goal

❖ Somebody who can offer encouragement when they need it

❖ Somebody who can compare them to the competition

❖ Somebody who can tell them what it takes to win

❖ Somebody who can tell them if they're about to fail, and

what it will take to change directions

Now substitute salespeople for athletes in the above explanation. How hard will I need to work to convince you that becoming an expert coach is essential for your success in management?

If You Sell

Let's face it. If Tiger Woods and Michael Jordan needed coaches, couldn't you benefit from one? What should you do? Ask for coaching help. Your persuasive argument is detailed in the bullets above. If you're not sure what you will be getting into, read the rest of this chapter before making your move. But let's be honest—after reading all the reasons above why coaching is essential, does it really matter what's involved? It's all about your (continued) success in sales. And by the way, if you're considering a future in sales management, you won't learn a more important skill than coaching and debriefing.

Debriefing

So, managers, where do you begin? An essential element of coaching is observing technique, in real time. Since that's not going to happen all the time with all of your salespeople, the next best thing is to conduct an effective debriefing of sales calls. Your plan needs to address the following:

1. Who needs debriefing?

2. When and how often do I do it?

3. How do I do it?

It's easy to say that everyone needs debriefing, at least occasionally. Obviously, some of your salespeople will need it more, and more frequently. Consider the graph below that plots your comfort and their effectiveness when they're "flying solo" on a sales call.

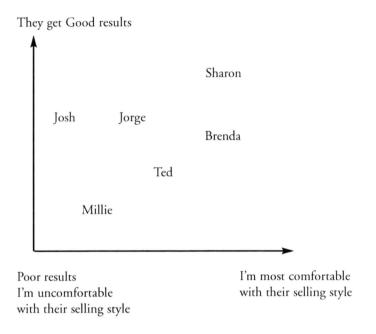

They get Good results

Sharon

Josh   Jorge
                    Brenda

              Ted

      Millie

Poor results   I'm most comfortable
I'm uncomfortable   with their selling style
with their selling style

Clearly Millie has the greatest need for debriefing. You can include any newly hired salespeople in her category.

Let's consider Josh. He gets results, but you're not comfortable with what he might be doing on his sales calls. Do you have salespeople like that? Perhaps they're loose cannons, who may sell but who sometimes upset clients or who may have an unorthodox selling approach that leaves you doubting.

Ted may be the salesperson who's always predictable— but a predictable C–, who's yet to grow to the next level. A word of caution here: Don't allow yourself to get too comfortable with salespeople who maintain an "average" performance. It's your responsibility to raise your bar so that "average" continuously means better performance. If you don't, you'll be treading water at best. Companies that don't consistently require growth from their people aren't successful in the long run. Regardless of what you think of Darwin's theory of evolution regarding the human race, it's highly accurate in describing the life cycle of companies. You change, adapt, and grow more efficiently and effectively over time, or you'll die out.

Back to your questions concerning debriefing: When and how often do I do it? A client who managed a staff of 15 salespeople in Atlanta complained to me in our first meeting, "There ain't enough of me for all of them." He was right. And this makes it even more important for managers to invest their time wisely if they are going to get results and stay sane.

Ideally you should debrief the salespeople who need it almost immediately after their sales calls. This isn't always feasible, for many obvious reasons. Let me suggest a strategy that has worked effectively.

Here's the ideal schedule for those on the preceding graph:

❖ New salespeople (Millie, in the chart above) should be debriefed daily.

❖ Underperforming (Ted) salespeople should be debriefed three times a week.

❖ Salespeople turning in a consistently average (Brenda) performance should be debriefed twice a week.

❖ Those who consistently perform at or above quota (Jorge) should be debriefed weekly.

❖ Stars (Sharon) should be debriefed periodically, say two or three times a month, but they must buy into it.

How often would you debrief Josh, your loose cannon who delivers results? Based on your comfort level with him (see graph), debrief him twice a week until you either get more comfortable or his consistency convinces you that you can cut back on the frequency.

You might be wondering why I don't suggest debriefing underperformers daily. That would be even more effective, but often isn't practical, especially if you have a large sales force or three or more underperformers. Remember that one of my objectives is for you to maintain your sanity.

If your sales staff is large, say more than 8 or 10 people, you probably have an assistant sales manager and group leaders. This will enable more debriefing to take place. Assuming you have one person in each of the first four categories, your debriefing weekly calendar would look like this:

M	T	W	TH	F
Millie	Millie	Millie	Millie	Millie
Ted	Josh	Ted	Jorge	Ted
Brenda	Sharon*	Brenda	Josh	

*This is one of Sharon's weeks to be debriefed.

☞ Key Thought

❖ Even if you assume 30 minutes for each debrief (and the average will be considerably less), on your three debrief days, you've only invested 90 minutes in this process.

Let's take a closer look at debriefing. You do it so:

❖ You can learn what happened on the sales call.

❖ You can learn what your salesperson thinks happened.

❖ Your salesperson learns what he did right and wrong.

❖ You can test for mind-reading and excuse-making.

❖ Your system of accountability becomes more visible.

❖ You learn more about how and if your salesperson is progressing.

❖ You send a clear message that you care about what and how your salesperson is doing.

All this enables you to:

❖ Forecast revenues more precisely.

❖ Predict more accurately an individual salesperson's success or failure.

❖ Understand where and how to help individual salespeople improve their results.

❖ Become a more successful sales manager.

The procedure:

1. Have explicit rules of engagement. Agree what is going to take place, for how long and how frequently, your right to point out what you observe as excuses or mind reading. An effective debriefing will usually run from 15 to 30 minutes, depending on how much coaching and teaching you're doing.

2. Salespeople must come prepared. Initially, they'll need to write down what happened, where they got stuck, what objections came up, and so forth.

3. Keep your salespeople in their Adult. If they get

emotional, call a time out and have them step back into analyzing, interpreting, thinking.

4. You stay away from your Critical Parent. Use your Nurturing Parent and your Adult.

5. The salespeople start with observed facts, and then move on to judgments.

6. Ask *How do you know that? and Why?* questions.

7. Always end the meeting with "lessons learned" and "action items."

8. Salespeople should grow from every debriefing. That means they are better at a specific strategy, tactic, or thought process than they were before.

Questions to ask:

❖ What were this client's expectations about this meeting?

❖ Did you have an agenda that the client agreed to ahead of time about what was to happen?

❖ As briefly as you can, tell me how the call went.

❖ On a 0 to 10 scale, where is the prospect? What are our chances of doing business?

❖ Tell my why you rated him as you did?

❖ What did the client say that stumped you? That posed an obstacle?

❖ When did this come up?

❖ When and how did he bring up competition?

❖ Where did you feel uncomfortable?

❖ How did you respond?

❖ If you had no fear of "going too far," and if you could rewind the tape, what would you have said? Asked?

❖ Let's role-play it now....

❖ What lessons did you learn from this sales call?

❖ How can you better prepare for next time?

❖ Who else needs to help you be more prepared?

Here's how it might play out:

You: Rick, I want to spend about 15 minutes debriefing what happened on the call to Thompson, Inc., yesterday.

Rick: OK.

You: Why don't we start, as we always do, with your overall rating. On a 0 to 10 scale, how did the meeting go?

Rick: I'd give it a 7.

You: And why a 7?

Rick: Well, we covered everything I'd planned for, but it could have gone better.

You: OK. Before we get into specifics about the call, let me ask you—it sounds like you had an agenda for the meeting, yes?

Rick: Sure, I always do.

You: And at what point did you share your agenda with your client?

Rick: I emailed Brad the topics I wanted to cover the day before, and I reiterated that 30 minutes should cover it...just as we've been practicing it in our sales meetings.

You: Excellent. I'm glad you've adopted this strategy. And Brad was OK with everything when you reviewed the agenda at the start of the meeting?

Rick: Yes, he was fine with it.

You: Tell me about the meeting. Was there any point where you didn't feel you were in control?

Rick: Well, everything went pretty well at the beginning. I covered the new research data about our response time, and how we compared favorably with the competition.

You: And how did Brad react?

Rick: He was really impressed! It was the first time I saw him smile, and his body language opened up.

You: Excellent! And even better that you noticed it! So what happened then?

Rick: Well, Brad brought up the fact that we haven't had much experience with companies and operating systems of his size, and he said that was a concern.

You: How did you feel when that happened?

Rick: Considering that his comment was accurate, that would have thrown anybody.

You: But how did you feel?

Rick: Lousy…at first, I didn't know what to say. I guess I didn't handle it as well as I could have. I told him how the principles are the same; our technical expertise is applied in the same way, no matter what the size of the operation might be.

You: And how did Brad react to your comments?

Rick: He didn't say much.

You: What did his body language tell you?

Rick: He was hard to read. After a minute, we moved on to installation schedules.

You: It sounds like you dropped out of your Adult and into your Child, if only for a moment. Would you agree?

Rick: Yes, that's pretty much what happened.

You: Feeling instead of thinking…not the best situation to be in?

Rick: Definitely not. But I did recover, almost immediately.

You: When you recovered, do you feel you were at your best?

Rick: Probably not. I was still a bit shaken up. This could be my biggest opportunity of the year, and I don't want to blow it.

You: I understand, and I agree with you. Let's try something here that could help. Let's rewind the tape of that meeting, back to the point where Brad made his comment. I'm Brad, and I've just finished stating my concern. You are in your Adult, you have no fear of losing the sale, and you're poised and calm. What would you say—how would you like to respond?

Rick: Well, I'd like to be able to tell the story of EMI, our customer that was acquired by that huge conglomerate Rippon three years ago, and how we were able to gear up to handle Rippon's entire system, and how satisfied they were.

You: Rick—at any point did you ask Brad how he viewed our competition in this light?

Rick: Actually, I didn't think to ask. I probably should have.

You: What might you have gained from asking?

Rick: Well, I know that two of our competitors have a lousy reputation when dealing with very large companies. It certainly would have been helpful to know if Brad was aware of it.

You: You're right. It might have taken some pressure off you. So let's role-play it now. The practice will help prepare you for success.

Rick: OK...

We could continue, but you get the picture. The manager learned several important things from this debrief:

❖ Rick initially rated the sales call too high.

❖ Rick lost his poise when he fell out of his Adult and into his Child, and thereby lost control.

❖ Rick needs practice in responding to tough situations, specifically those instances when he's faced with a large potential client who's concerned that EMI hasn't worked with very large companies before.

❖ The time to give Rick the practice he needs is right now.

As you debrief regularly, you're giving your salespeople the best chance to become more successfully. Be careful!—debriefings that don't deal with specifics aren't worth much, either to you or your salespeople. Considering all the reasons you want to debrief that we mentioned a few pages ago, you must direct your conversations down to the details.

Consistency

Everyone wants more consistent results, and this comes only from consistent reinforcement of good strategies. By conducting regular debriefing sessions you:

1. Begin to close the gap between where they are and where you need them to be, or

2. Find out quickly if your salesperson is not going to grow or become successful (enough) with you.

After all, isn't either outcome an improvement?

I ask managers the following question when I begin working with them: "If a salesperson is not going to be successful with you, when do you want to find out?" Invariably they answer: "Right now!"

My follow-up question is: "Are you doing everything possible to find out as soon as possible if he or she is going to fail?" You can guess what their answer is: "No." There are two main reasons for this:

1. They have no system in place to help determine in short order if someone will fail.

2. They don't want to confront this situation, and then have to start the recruiting, hiring, training, hoping, etc. that follow employee turnover.

Let's review the conversation we just quoted in TA terms,

that is, as a transaction.

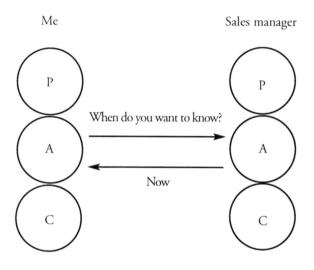

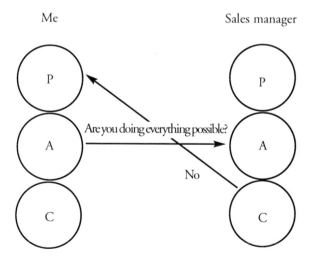

Most managers become "not-OK" when they hear my second question. They feel caught, found out, less worthy, even guilty. This is not my intent (at least not completely). My objective is for them to consider their answer and the impact it's having on their overall sales effort. If you're like most sales managers, you've delayed taking action with an underperforming salesperson that wasn't going to change. The financial and emotional costs can be overwhelming when you take time to add them up. My objective here is to get you to buy into the necessity of regularly debriefing your people. You can't afford not to do it.

The Return on Your Investment

Let's face it, you're always asking yourself, *Is all this worth it?* After all, like the man said, *There ain't enough of you for all of them.* So where will you get your best return on your debriefing investment?

As enjoyable as it is to spend time with your top salespeople, they don't need (or want) this process. Also this is the group that probably has the smallest growth potential, because they're the closest to maxing out their time and resources. If your top salesperson is at 150 percent of quota, she isn't going to double her production, even with your help.

What about those at the bottom of the scale? In most cases, they have so many problems and weaknesses—and they're in their Child so often—you're not likely to see enough growth. Devoting part of each day with three failing salespeople, only to see one improve to the level of mediocrity after a year, while the other two fail, is a poor investment. So here's my point: You might debrief them daily for a few weeks, but soon it will become clear to everyone what the future holds. This kind of intense sales management doesn't go on forever. Salespeople either show real signs of growth or they fall out. Clearly every hour you spend with a salesperson who's failing is time taken from a mediocre performer with real growth potential. Your meter is always running, and you should be calculating your return on investment continuously.

By the way, how often have you heard people complain that they don't want to be micromanaged? This term has acquired a bad rap when it actually should have positive connotations. Effective management focuses on specifics—actions, mindsets, attitudes, fears, beliefs, needs, questions, and so on. If you're not concerned with these particulars, your efforts won't produce much change. Most salespeople who complain about being micromanaged haven't been managed enough, and that's one reason they and you need to pay attention to specifics.

It's the group in the middle of the pack, if they aren't making excuses, where you should be investing the biggest portion of your time. Many in this group could double their production and still have room for growth. Every one that grows into a solid producer widens the path for the rest of your staff. They are the ones whose growth is most believable and inspiring to the rest of the middle group, because most people can identify with them. As your C and D players become B players, morale will improve and your company will become a magnet for others like them. Build your company's (and your own) reputation as a place where people grow, and your revenues will mushroom.

Role-Playing

When I was 12 years old I loved to play baseball. One game still stands out in my mind. I was batting in the bottom of the last inning with two outs and two men on base. We trailed by a run, and I felt pressure to deliver. I had pretty good reflexes for a 12-year-old, and I rarely struck out. After fouling off a couple of pitches, I took two balls outside. Then the pitcher threw one right at my head. It was only my quick reflexes that saved me, as I dived away from the plate and onto the ground. As I landed in the dust with a thud, I heard the umpire call, "Strike three, you're out!" That was my introduction to a real curve ball.

Without batting practice, the first curve balls your salespeople will see will come from their clients and prospects. And your salespeople will strike out. Repeated role-playing in a wide variety of selling scenarios is the best preparation they can have.

Because you're responsible for fielding the best-prepared team you can, your sales staff needs to be prepared to hit every kind of pitch that's thrown to them. If they are surprised by what a client throws at them, what does that say about your preparation?

I get three basic objections from managers when I bring up role-playing:

1. It takes too much time.

2. My people aren't comfortable doing it.

3. I'm not comfortable (i.e., skilled enough) doing it.

Interestingly, the one complaint I never hear from managers is that role-playing doesn't work. It does. You know it. So do your salespeople.

Let's address these three objections.

Too much time. Learning involves two complementary behaviors—taking information in and giving it out. A baseball player wouldn't expect to learn how to hit a curve ball just from listening to lectures and watching videos, would he? A salesperson can listen to a tape on asking questions for hours, and he still won't develop much expertise unless he hears himself asking those questions in a simulated sales call. If you make role-playing a part of your debriefing sessions where the opportunity naturally arises, you'll find that your time investment won't be excessive. It will also save you time on the back end discussing why your salespeople were unprepared for what happened, and why they bailed out.

They aren't comfortable. Of course they aren't! First of all, they're not comfortable because they haven't done it often enough. (The second and third times I saw a curve ball weren't much easier for me. After about a hundred curves, I stopped bailing out of the batter's box.) In addition, your people probably don't want to look bad in front of you. But would you rather they fail in front of you or in front of a client, where they can lose a sale or an account? Their discomfort comes from their Child. It's your responsibility to help them understand—in their Adult—why role-playing is an insurance policy to increase their chances of being in control, of not being surprised, and of getting the outcomes they want from every sales call. Members of many professions must have continuing professional education (CPE) to maintain and upgrade their knowledge and skills. Your salespeople need to view role-playing as required CPE to upgrade their own professional skills.

They still won't like it much at first. But as they get better and stronger from it, many will learn to enjoy it. We all tend to enjoy doing things we're good at, and we don't enjoy doing things we don't do well. Winning is more fun than losing, even in preparation.

You aren't comfortable. There are probably a couple of reasons for this. First, you probably have little experience with role-playing. Second, you may not know how to conduct an effective role-play. Some key points to remember:

❖ You don't have to have all the answers. If you have good questions, you can help your salespeople discover the answers for themselves.

❖ You won't feel the pressure if you play the part of the client or prospect.

❖ When you take on the role of salesperson, you don't have to be perfect. In most instances, you'll have no problem coming up with better responses than your salespeople used.

❖ Because you're not as emotionally involved with their sales calls as they tend to be, your objectivity will enable you to see solutions they've missed.

❖ Nobody is supposed to be perfect. Role-playing is nothing more than an opportunity to get better at a specific thought process, behavior or technique. It's just good practice.

☞ **Key Thought**

❖ Role-playing is preparing to win. Without it you're preparing to lose.

You want your salespeople to be open to this process—their defenses lowered—in their Adult and out of their Child, and ready to learn. Here are some comments you can make that they'll find helpful:

❖ *You're not allowed to get this right the first few times, OK?*

❖ *Remember, we're practicing this because you're not perfect yet. If you were, we wouldn't need to practice it.*

❖ *Let's see how it plays out and what we can learn from it.*

❖ *It's fine not to be comfortable. This is how you get comfortable.*

❖ *I want you uncomfortable now and working through it, so you'll be more comfortable with anything that happens the next time you're in front of your client.*

❖ *It's fine to mess up here in front of me. You won't lose a sales or a commission here.*

❖ *We're going to do what we can to make sure you don't get surprised or lose control when you're on that sales call tomorrow.*

Michael Jordan is known throughout the world for being the best basketball player who ever lived. His teammates on the Chicago Bulls knew something else about him that most fans didn't: He was also the best practice player who ever lived. His teammate Scottie Pippin said that after practicing with Michael, the games were easy because they were so well prepared for anything that could come up. They practiced so hard they were confident in their ability to win any game, no matter how many points behind they were. Even the opposing teams came share this belief, which made them even tougher to defeat. For several years the Bulls were almost invincible. Make sure that your salespeople make the connection between practice and success.

I've often thought that the average plumber or electrician who comes to your house is better prepared than the average salesperson. Your salespeople need to be far better than average.

The Fast Track: Tape Your Role-Plays

Here's how to use videotaping with (almost) no effort on your part:

1. Tape the role-play.

2. Then you tell the salesperson, "Review the tape, note any areas where you can improve, and then call me when you're ready to tape a better version."

3. Repeat step #1.

4. Repeat step #2.

5. Ask the salesperson to let you know when she's ready for you to view the tape.

6. When she's ready, you watch together, take notes, and discuss.

7. You may need one more version to fine-tune.

8. Note that you can provide feedback at any time, especially if you sense they need help in a particular spot.

9. You can ask other sales reps to help. They can sub for you in step #4.

This puts the responsibility for improvement where it belongs: on the salesperson. I've seen many instances where the manager says almost nothing during the process, and yet the salesperson improves dramatically by the second or third takes.

I'm often asked about the effectiveness of playing a video-taped role-play in front of the entire sales staff. It's entertaining and can be beneficial for some people, but many find it an unsafe environment. There's usually lots of poking fun and joking, while the individual on tape feels extremely not-OK and defensive. If you do choose this method, tell your group that everyone will be on video, so if you take cheap shots, they'll come back at you. Once people get used to the procedure, the ribbing subsides and you can make some progress.

Here's a twist that produces good, competitive results: Save the best role-plays over two weeks and then play a selection of these takes at your sales meeting for discussion. This will become a kind of academy awards event, with people vying for their moment of fame.

Here's how to use audiotaping with (almost) no effort on your part:

1. If people are working on phone technique, whether they're making sales calls or prospecting calls, have them call you and tape the call.

2. Have them listen to the tape, and set up a time for them to call you back for a second effort, which you also tape.

3. When they're ready for you to hear a "best practice" version, you'll listen.

4. Any time you can give feedback before they listen to the tape will help them refine their listening and learning.

5. You can play these tapes at sales meetings just as we discussed with the video sessions.

6. Save the best tapes and use them as training for new salespeople you train in the future. In this way you develop a library of "best practices" tapes for new hires to listen to and model, without using any of your time.

Chapter 8

Recruiting New Salespeople

Does This Candidate Have What I'm Looking For?

One obvious way to improve your sales force is by adding new blood. Here's the problem: Every seven quarts of new blood you hire comes with attitudes, beliefs, and fears. Salespeople always bring their Child and their not-OK feelings with them. That's why you must become skilled at evaluating the candidate's mindset.

When was the last time you interviewed a candidate who said, "You know, I'm a pretty good salesperson, except that I really can't handle rejection, I desperately need people to like me, I'm intimidated quite easily, and if you put pressure on me, I tend to fold." Nobody will volunteer this information, but take heart: You definitely will uncover all these problems and more if you hire the person and observe him carefully for 45 to 60 days. Can we agree this would be an awful recruiting strategy?

Good. So stop using it!

In keeping with my tendency to make lists, below is a recipe for an interviewing strategy to prevent you from hiring the candidate we just described. We can title this one *Knowing What You Want...Before You Start Looking:*

1. Make a list of what you want the successful candidate to have, to do, and to be—this includes qualities as well as skills.

2. Prioritize these skills by group A or B. A = must have, can't do without. (Caution: This shouldn't be an extensive wish list, because the ideal candidate who possesses everything you want probably wouldn't take the job.) Consider the skills your top salespeople share. Keep the list short. B = desirable, but you're willing to develop later or live without them if the candidate has the skills in group A.

Here's a sample list you can use for what to look for in a closer. A closer:

❖ Takes control of sales situation

❖ Qualifies well

❖ Uses a sequential selling system

❖ Knows our market

❖ Knows our industry

❖ Knows our products/services

❖ Knows our customers

❖ Has good rapport skills

❖ Is comfortable calling at the top

❖ Has done a lot of prospecting

❖ Has prospected in our market

❖ Has prospected to our clients

❖ Knows what to do with objections

- ❖ Sells with intellect (Adult and Nurturing Parent)
- ❖ Is in control of emotions (stays out of Child)
- ❖ Has already earned an acceptable level of income
- ❖ Uncovers how decision will be made
- ❖ Doesn't take stalls or put-offs
- ❖ Asks good questions in an appropriate manner
- ❖ Remains poised under pressure
- ❖ Is rejection-proof
- ❖ Has the ability to get a person talking and opening up
- ❖ Does whatever it takes to get the job done
- ❖ Thrives in a fast paced environment
- ❖ Works well in chaos
- ❖ Follows directions well
- ❖ Is good with details
- ❖ Can delegate the details
- ❖ Is a team player
- ❖ Is independent
- ❖ Has been successful without much training
- ❖ Has been successful with little structure
- ❖ Has been successful with little hands-on management
- ❖ Has good time management skills
- ❖ Has family role models for sales success
- ❖ Has family role models for dealing with top-level decision makers
- ❖ Is an extrovert; a socializer
- ❖ Is someone you would enjoy socializing with after work

3. Develop questions that identify whether or not your candidate has the skills you're looking for.

Ask these questions in every interview, and rate the candidate's answers. I use the following ratings: 1 = cause for concern, investigate further, a weaknesses; 2 = OK, acceptable; 3 = a strength

4. Assuming you're looking for the same skills in each interview, you can now compare numerical scores among candidates.

Regardless of whether or not you use an outside evaluation/testing service, you will now have a more objective approach to evaluating sales candidates. You can quantify as you qualify each candidate in key areas.

I can't tell you what personal qualities you will want in your next salesperson, because that's so subjective. However, the skills you're seeking are more predictable. When interviewing salespeople I'm trying to uncover if they:

1. Remain poised under pressure

2. Can handle rejection

3. Know what to do with objections

4. Try to close in an appropriate manner

5. Qualify well

6. Control interview by getting me talking

7. Take stalls or put-offs

8. Present information logically and clearly

Although you may be looking for additional skills, these eight probably should make your "A List." Evaluating every candidate on these categories provides you with a basis for comparison. Since on my 1 to 3 scale a perfect score would be 24, how excited should you get about someone who only scores 10 to 12? Using this kind of system you can now more objectively compare a candidate you interviewed three weeks ago with one you saw this morning. Less subjectivity and more standardization will produce better hires.

Note that the first two skills I've listed above are essentially about remaining in the Adult instead of defaulting to the Child—staying intellectually involved but not emotionally overshadowed. In most selling situations there is no more important skill for a salesperson to demonstrate. And if he doesn't bring it to the sales call, he's unlikely to find it when confronted by a tough client.

What's an acceptable score or range for the candidate you want to hire? Experience will tell you this. Rate your current salespeople on these eight skills, and then look at the scores of those who are successful. Of course, the job, your company, your compensation plan, and other factors may be preventing you from attracting the candidates you want to hire. I've seen many companies looking to hire a salesperson who scores at least a 20, but it's for a position that's attractive only to someone with a mid-teens score.

Many managers have favorite questions they routinely ask. Unfortunately, when I inquire what they're hoping to uncover with these questions, they rarely have a good answer. Managers ask the same questions often out of habit. The problem is that this habit doesn't help them achieve their objective: distinguishing between those candidates who will succeed and those who won't.

I also have some favorite questions, and they're based eliciting information about some these eight skill categories. See if you can identify which categories I'm testing for in the questions below. The answers follow at the end.

1. *Gina, before we get started today, can I assume your selling skills and expertise will be on display in this interview?*

2. *Almost every candidate I interview gives me that kind of answer. Would you like to try again?*

3. *Gina, closing is a very important part of our business, as you might imagine. How would you rate yourself on this vital skill, say, on a 0 to 10 scale, with 10 being the highest?... That's good. And you understand that you're in a selling situation now with me, yes?...So then, how are you going to close me?* (Now shut up, look serious, and maintain eye contact with her.)

4. *We find that the ability to read prospects in a face-to-face selling situation is essential to selling success. How would you rate yourself in that skill?...Good. Tell me how you're reading me so far in this interview....Why did you rate it as you did?*

5. *Why haven't you made more money in your past jobs?* (Whatever she says, shake your head and look down at your notes, pausing to give her time to remark on your body language. Then write something on your paper, as if you are critiquing her.)

The previous questions enable me to score the candidate on most of the eight skills from my list.

Skill Numbers

Question	From My List
One	3, 2, 1
Two	1
Three	1, 6, 5
Four	1, 6, 5, 8
Five	2, 1, 8

Note that these questions and interactions don't allow the candidate to intellectualize the situation. You don't want Gina to discuss how she would handle a difficult prospect. Instead you become that prospect and observe her responses, when she has something to lose (as in a sales call). You will learn more about your candidates from this kind of interview than you ever imagined.

☞ Key Thoughts

❖ Begin every candidate interview with your end results in mind.

❖ As the qualities and skills you seek to identify change over time, you'll adjust the categories and questions to fit.

This approach will help to ensure that the infusion of new blood to your sales force won't require an emergency transfusion 90 days later.

Chapter 9

Bringing a New Hire Up to Speed

For Their Benefit and Yours

In the 1970s I worked as a salesman for one of the leading printing companies in Atlanta. We were extremely profitable and—not coincidentally—lean in terms of management as well. After I'd been there for about a couple of years, one morning a young man came into my office at 8:30 and introduced himself: "Hi, I'm Sam, and I'm the new trainee." After a minute or two of small talk, I wished him well and went back to what I'd been doing. About 15 minutes later, I noticed that he had made his way down the hall, introducing himself at each office, spending as much time as people would allow.

At 10 a.m. I had to meet with my boss Ed to discuss a key account. After we were done, I asked about Sam and his role in the company. Ed explained that the owner of the company had liked Sam and had hired him in the belief that he would be able to add value somewhere, some time down the road. As we spoke, it was apparent Ed knew this was a mistake. Finally, I said, "Ed, Sam says he's a trainee. Doesn't having a train-ee imply the existence of a train-er? And a training program?"

Sam's first day was his last. Because we had no structure in place to help him become successful, it was unfair to everyone to keep him around. If you don't have a systematic approach to bring new hires on board and get them productive quickly, you aren't doing your job. The new hire will suffer, and so will you and your company. Like everything else we've discussed, it's not rocket science. Too often sales managers realize they have to "get serious" with a new salesperson who has made little progress after he has been on board for 30 to 60 days. In most cases the other salespeople aren't surprised at this outcome, because many of them have lived through the same process.

Optimum New Hire Training

Your company pays all new salespeople their guaranteed base in the first 60 to 90 days, regardless of how well they're doing. Let's look at the keys to securing a better and quicker return on this investment.

I'm sure you'll agree that your new hires:

❖ Are highly motivated to succeed from the very beginning

❖ Want to make a good impression, and quickly

❖ Want to look good and earn praise from you

❖ Learn best within some structure instead of through osmosis

❖ Can master only one or two skills at a time

❖ Learn more effectively through application to real life selling situations than through abstract intellectual ideas

Let's use this information to help get your new sales-person—we'll call her Jessica—up to speed more quickly. Here's our strategy:

1. Using the following categories, list the knowledge you want Jessica to master. Your categories might look something like this:

❖ Product knowledge and industry knowledge

❖ Our competition—how we stack up

❖ Sales technique

❖ Company policy and procedures (I can't help here)

2. After you've filled out the key information and skills under each heading, prioritize each item—1, 2, and 3, with 1 being a top priority and on down. Don't spend time evaluating whether a particular item should be given a 2 or a 3.

3. Now it's time to create questions or situations so Jessica can practice and master this knowledge in a role-play scenario. For example, if you want her to be able to talk intelligently about how you offer more value than your major competitor, create a question that forces her to respond with that information.

4. Starting with the priority level 1 knowledge, you will be giving Jessica daily homework assignments that she will prepare for the next business day. You can start with one assignment at the end of each day, and as she grows in knowledge and confidence—perhaps after a week or two—increase the load to two assignments each night.

5. The most important element in this program is that Jessica must be prepared to take her "oral exam" on the previous day's assignment every day. This means she's doing some homework on her own time from her first day on the

job. By the way, we've even given assignments to new hires a week before they started the job, and they arrived on the first day confidently ahead of the game.

6. You may not be available to give Jessica her oral examination or to role-play with her every morning. No problem: She leaves her answers, explanations, presentations on your voicemail. You can give her feedback after you've had a chance to listen. Your voicemail system is one of the most powerful pieces of technology in your company, but very few managers utilize it for training purposes.

7. By the second or third week you should be able to combine this process with the videotaping and audiotaping procedures we discussed in the last chapter.

8. Have team leaders or senior sales reps periodically assume your role in this process. Everyone will benefit from a change in the cast.

9. Still too much work for you? Involve the rest of your sales team! Give them the categories, and ask them to each come up with three to five important pieces of information for each one. You can even have them place an asterisk by the items that they feel especially confident about, on which they'd be willing to work with Jessica. Now everyone is involved in her success.

10. Pay attention to the kinds of assignments Jessica finds difficult or challenging. This is a good predictor of the kinds of selling situations that she'll have trouble handling when she's on her own.

This approach to developing new salespeople does several things for you:

❖ The new hire (Jessica) focuses on priority issues immediately.

❖ She takes much of the responsibility for getting up to speed.

❖ You provide the structure necessary for continued learning to take place.

❖ You're able to receive and give instant feedback on how your new person is doing. Jessica won't be able to get too far off course without your knowledge. This daily feedback loop makes everything easier and faster.

❖ By spreading the work and responsibility for learning among your sales team, more of them become invested in the success of new people.

❖ You are holding Jessica accountable from her first day for mastering specific, relevant knowledge essential to her success.

❖ No surprises! You won't be surprised at some point that she can't handle X or discuss Y on a sales call.

Often a manager will ask me, "How soon should I expect Jessica to be productive?" Well, what do you mean by "productive"? Specifically, what do you want or need her do, and how well must she do it? Some possible answers could include:

❖ Respond to a prospect who sincerely wants to know how you are better than a competitor

❖ Respond to a prospect who sincerely wants to know why you are priced higher than his current supplier

❖ Respond to a prospect who says he's satisfied with his current supplier

❖ Getting _____ face-to-face meetings with clients and prospects

❖ Averaging _____ appointments for at least three consecutive weeks

❖ Booking _____ of qualified second appointments per week

❖ Generating _____ qualified proposals per _____

❖ Running sales calls where he or she is in charge

❖ Running sales calls independently

❖ Bringing in _____ sales or $ per week for three consecutive weeks

You're shortchanging Jessica if your answers are just limited to:

❖ I'm feeling better about her.

❖ She seems to be "getting it."

❖ She's no longer asking rookie questions.

❖ She seems more confident.

❖ She says her pipeline is beginning to fill up.

These five answers are much too subjective to measure. And although they can be factors in your assessment about Jessica's progress, they don't provide you with a complete picture.

Keys to successful development of new salespeople:

1. Develop objective benchmarks in advance.

2. Let your new salesperson know that these are your expectations of her.

3. Establish "red flags" that signal real problems, and make sure you know how to recognize them.

4. Monitor and coach her regularly. Too often managers start this process two or three times a week with a new hire, then quickly find other, "more pressing" tasks that cause them to work less frequently with her. The result is that the discussions become less specific and less useful. You end up getting surprised at some point when she's really off track.

5. Hold her accountable for specific actions, strategies, attitudes, and knowledge.

6. It's helpful to have one other person with whom you can discuss and get feedback about her progress. This can be a senior sales rep whose opinion you value, another manager or even an outside consultant or coach.

7. Learning new information should mostly involve the new hire's time. When she's ready to give out this information, you'll invest your time.

Below is a scheduled outline for Jessica's progress in her first two weeks with your company, including what she must accomplish as well as the managing help she will receive.

By the end of week one:

❖ Be able to give a three- to five-minute briefing to a new prospect about the typical problems we help clients solve. (We'll delve more deeply into this sales approach in a later chapter.)

❖ Be able to answer a prospect's questions about our three major competitors, differentiating us among them.

—Jessica masters content of chapters 1 through 4 in our sales manual, which address her two assignments for the week.

—Jessica meets daily with sales manager for role-play 20 minutes.

—Jessica meets daily (10 to 15 minutes) with either Sandy or Robert (senior sales reps) for their input on the topics above.

—Every day Jessica records on voicemail her three- to five-minute briefing. At least one person cited above should listen and provide feedback.

By the end of week two:

❖ Jessica masters content in chapters five through eight of the sales manual.

❖ She demonstrates competency in making a cold call and closing for a face-to-face appointment. She audiotapes two role-play scenarios and reviews them for the next day.

❖ She demonstrates competency responding to prospect's question about competitive strengths. Friday role-play to be videotaped.

—She makes cold calls daily on two sales reps and one manager in our company, receives feedback and revises approach as needed.

—She role-plays at least twice daily with sales reps/managers and confronts price objections.

—She reviews tapes daily in preparation for Friday's "exam."

If you are giving Jessica daily homework assignments that address these skills, won't she be more successful at the end of her second week with you than any recent new hire? If you plan ahead for the progress she needs to make, you'll avoid the painful experience of "starting over" with her 30 days later. Remember the guy on the old oil change commercial: "You can pay me now, or pay me later."

Chapter 10

Motivating Your Sales Staff

Clearing the Ever-Higher Bar

I have a couple of salespeople who seem to lose their motivation, and their production is all peaks and valleys. I've talked to them about consistency, but it doesn't help.

If somebody isn't really motivated, there's nothing you can do.

We have quarterly contests to motivate our salespeople, but few of them get excited or motivated by them.

What will it take to motivate my people?

These are some concerns and frustrations I hear around motivating salespeople. In the dictionary under motivate you'll find, "to provide with an incentive; to move to action; to impel." For our purposes let's define motivation as the state in which a salesperson, for his own reasons, demonstrates the consistent energy and focus to achieve his own goals, exceeding those you've set for him.

Sound like a tall order? High standards begin with

definitions. We don't gain much by dumbing them down or lowering the bar.

From your experience you know that people buy for their reasons, not necessarily yours. This also holds true for your salespeople. Based on their own agenda and beliefs, they may buy into your required levels of activity, the risk-taking actions you demand like prospecting and closing, and even you're your goals and philosophy of doing business. Or they may not. Let's take a closer look at what's going on with your salespeople.

Unfortunately too few people have their own goals and objectives firmly in place, with specific timelines for achievement. And fewer still have them in writing. Why? Why is it that people you ask will tell you they have goals, but the goals are in their head? If they answered honestly, they'd tell you, "If I don't put them in writing, then I have a fall-back position when I don't achieve them: I really didn't mean it! I wasn't committed. I wasn't going all out. I didn't really fail." It's the Child wanting to play it safe, fingers crossed behind his back. Nowadays it's called a free do-over. As long as they don't have something in writing with a date by it, they can rationalize to themselves (and anyone else) that they're still working on it, or that they've changed their mind about that particular objective.

You might think that salespeople would be different from the general population, but my experience is that they aren't. They may talk a better game, especially if they sense that's what you want to hear from them, but the reality is that most are reacting to today's situations, this month's challenges, this quarter's requirements. Salespeople certainly seem to have dreams and fantasies, based on future commission checks, but that's far from having established goals. And if they don't have their own specific personal goals, they certainly don't have a way to track their progress towards them, or a support group for encouragement. In other words, they aren't really motivated toward any specific achievement. This doesn't mean they can't be successful, especially if they buy into your goals or the corporate objectives. This often happens with salespeople: They lack their own personal reasons for success, and it's usually simpler to adopt yours, at least for a while.

Pop Quiz

It's time for a quiz. (If you get even one answer wrong, you fail!) Consider the following scenario: You have a choice of managing two different sales staffs. Group A is comprised of people who have their own clear, specific reasons for their success. They are committed to achieving their goals and know what they need to do to make this happen. They will track their progress and have significant people in their lives who support their efforts.

Group B has the same number of salespeople, but they lack their own goals and objectives. They might have dreams and wishes but nothing too specific and no timeline. Commitment really isn't there because there's nothing to which to be committed. They may adopt your goals temporarily, but then again they may not. Time will tell.

Below are the test questions. Circle the correct letter for your answer.

❖ Which group will be more motivated? A or B

❖ Which group will work harder? A or B

❖ Which group will work longer? A or B

❖ Which group will stretch beyond their comfort zone to excel? A or B

- ❖ Which group will be lower maintenance for you? A or B
- ❖ Which group will be more fun to manage? A or B
- ❖ Which group will be more exciting to manage? A or B
- ❖ Which group will produce greater revenue? A or B
- ❖ Which group will produce greater profits? A or B
- ❖ Which group will make fewer excuses? A or B
- ❖ Which group will bring you greater satisfaction? A or B

You had no trouble finding the right answer to each question. So here's one more question for you: Are you now convinced of the need for your sales staff to be committed to and excited about their own goals?

Remember Tamara from the high-tech firm back in the introduction? Now it's time to help her achieve some consistency. People aren't motivated for long by goals they've inherited or been assigned. Outstanding motivational speaker Zig Ziglar asks the question in his goal-setting programs, *Would you rather be a wandering generality or a meaningful specific?* You know the choice you want your salespeople to make.

Let's take a closer look at goals. I've taken almost a dozen goal-setting programs, both live and on tape over the years. They all work and have much in common. In the following pages I've distilled what I believe is the best and most workable approach you can use with any size staff. The only requirement for it to work is that your people have the ability to earn more money by selling more. Ready?

Let's begin with an acronym: SMART. You have a valid goal if it is:

S = specific

M = measurable

A = achievable

R = realistic

T = time frame

For example, if you want to get in shape or be a better runner, these don't meet the criteria for valid goals. Let's get more specific:

S = You want to run a mile in under seven minutes.

M= It's certainly trackable.

A = Is it achievable? Well, others certainly have achieved it.

R = Is it realistic? If your best time is eight and one-half minutes, and you ran it two years ago, we can probably say this goal is realistic.

T = Now you need a time frame. If it's now March and you want to hit this goal by August 1 of this year, you've met all the requirements. If, on the other hand, your deadline is April 15 of this year, your goal is no longer realistic.

Now for the actual exercise that you'll be conducting for your staff: Remember, we're going through this to help your salespeople will become more motivated, so they and you are more successful. Don't lose sight of the big picture as we dive into the details.

As your salespeople get excited about and committed to achieving their own goals, your job will change—and for the better. You're going to be less of a taskmaster and more of a goals attainment coach, and you'll encounter less resistance to your efforts.

There are some materials you'll need for the goal-setting exercise we're about to detail. They include:

❖ Lots of 8½-inch by 11-inch notebook paper

❖ A 2-foot by 3-foot poster board for each salesperson

❖ Several dispensers of scotch tape

❖ Scissors for each salesperson

❖ Magazines (They can each bring 5 to 10 from home. They should contain pictures of things that are important in their lives, like travel, homes, kitchens, cars, scuba diving, etc.)

Here we go:

1. Under the following categories, write down everything you want in the next 12 months. Don't consider how practical they are. Just write as many things as you can, as fast as you can. Let your imagination run free. You have five minutes for this part of the exercise.

2. Now take a careful look at which columns are loaded and which are sparsely populated. Take a couple of minutes more to fill in the blanks.

3. (Tell your staff) It's going to be important that for the rest of this program you are supportive of one another. No criticizing, no undercutting of anybody. You're all going to have an opportunity to share your goals in front of the group. (Those who live in their Critical Parent will be the ones who have trouble with this, as opposed to those with a strong Nurturing Parent.)

TOYS	FAMILY	TRAVEL	KNOWLEDGE

4. Now, in turn, you'll each stand up and read what you've written under each column. This is so everyone can get ideas from one another.

5. Next step: Select the most important goal for each category and underline it.

6. Now you're each going to write a solid paragraph, up to a page long, about why you are going to achieve each goal that you've underlined. During this exercise you'll answer the following questions: (15 minutes for this part)

❖ How will I feel when I've achieved this goal?

❖ How will I see myself?

❖ How will my family and friends see me?

❖ What will this say about my abilities?

❖ How will this affect my reputation in my personal life?

❖ How will this affect my reputation in my professional life?

❖ What fears will I have overcome during this process?

❖ How will I have grown?

❖ What will I have learned about myself?

Make sure you answer all these questions in your paragraph about each goal. This writing process is how you are going to sell yourself on achieving your goals. Or not. If you can't come up with enough reasons to hit your target, you'll probably give up before you're successful. That's why you're doing this with the goal you want most in each category.

7. The next step is to find pictures of their goals in the magazines on hand, cut them out and tape them to their poster board. Let them spend as much time as they want on this step.

8. Now it's time to figure out what your investment will

be for each of the goals you've written about. You will have to invest:

❖ Time

❖ Money

❖ Energy

❖ Some risk—perhaps getting outside your comfort zone, trying something new, getting better at something you're already doing, and so forth

It's important now to break down the investment, especially the money part, into monthly and weekly parts. Some things they want will be financed and paid for monthly. They probably look at their sales activities weekly. You'll also have to remind the group that they're investing after tax dollars. If somebody needs an extra $5,000 to pay for one of her goals, and she's in a 30 percent tax bracket, she'll need about $7,500 in extra commissions to fund it. This can be a sobering experience.

9. Underneath each picture of a goal they should write down their estimate of the investment it will take.

10. Important note: You need to understand the psychological process that you've led them through up to this point. As they came up with those things they wanted, and then wrote down their how they would feel when they got it, their Child ego state was quite active. Now as they are doing the accounting for what they want, their Adult has taken over. If you see heads starting to shake or depressed faces as they add up the money they're going to need, it's important that you get their Parent involved, and you'll do this with your own Parent: "Hey, you just came up with all sorts of great reasons why you're going be successful. Aren't they still good reasons? (The only place where success comes before work is in the dictionary.) Aren't you ready to be successful?"

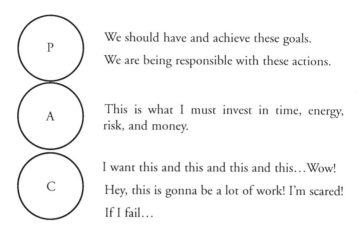

We should have and achieve these goals.
We are being responsible with these actions.

This is what I must invest in time, energy, risk, and money.

I want this and this and this and this...Wow!
Hey, this is gonna be a lot of work! I'm scared!
If I fail...

11. Ask them who in their personal life needs to know about these goals? Who is in a position to offer them support—emotional and financial? Who will be a cheerleader for them? Ask them if they've thought of *you*! If not, they should write your name down as a key person in their camp. Ask them which ego state is going to determine their success over the next year. You might want to remind the group of something I mentioned in my introduction about successful people. They are the ones who have made a habit of doing the things that unsuccessful people are unwilling to do. This is another way of saying that successful people control the not-OK, frightened Child inside them so it can celebrate success after the Adult and Parent have done the work.

12. Now it's time to turn the money they need into sales made, new clients acquired, additional deals done—whatever your business model is. An average new sale or client is worth _____ in your business. How many additional new clients will they need to get everything they wrote about?

13. Once they have that number, they now need to turn these new clients into additional activities: proposals, meetings, first appointments, phone calls—they break down new

business into the step by step processes you use, with corresponding ratios of one step to the next.

14. As the days and weeks unfold, you'll be framing many of your comments to them in the context of reaching their goals. For example, Melody's main goal was to spend 10 days in Paris studying impressionist painting, which she hadn't done since college 15 years earlier. Here are some comments we made to her as she went to work on getting the money for her vacation:

—Melody, you said you want two full days at the Marmottan (filled with Monet paintings) Museum. That's roughly 20 percent of your stay in Paris. Have you figured out which of your clients is going to be paying for that with the sales you make to him?

—Melody, to fly business class instead of coach is only $900…we're talking two additional average-sized orders before the end of the month to book it. Do you know how much more comfortable this trip is going to be in business class?

—Melody, I know you're planning on visiting Giverny to see Monet's gardens. Are you aware that you can hire a private coach to take you and provide an individualized tour? Here's the brochure. I think you have an existing client who might be willing to fund that by upgrading to our new system with us.

We regularly placed pictures and articles in front of her that kept her excitement (Child) level high, and encouraged her every time she hit her weekly goals. At sales meetings every couple of weeks people enjoyed asking her how much closer she had come to earning her trip. When she reached her financial goal—five weeks before her vacation was to begin—we had a pre–bon voyage party for her. A couple of weeks later Melody came into the office with a look of exaltation on her face. When asked what was going on, she said that she'd just closed a large sale that was going to pay for two full days of "the most knowledgeable personal guide on impressionism in Paris." She hadn't mentioned this on her "wish list" about Paris, because the extra cost was really going to be a stretch for her. Melody didn't stop working and selling until the day before she left for Paris. She'd had her best six months of production by far in her nine years with the company, and she announced to everyone that the following year she'd be vacationing in Florence and Rome for two weeks. Think she was motivated?

I'd like to tell you that everybody who goes through this exercise is going to develop enough sustained drive and commitment to reach the next level of success, but you know that won't happen. Let's face it—no strategy works 100 percent of the time. But if you can help even half your people grow to levels they hadn't seriously considered before, isn't that strategy worthwhile?

Achieving our goals. strengthens our confidence to reach higher goals next time. Growth doesn't stop with success. Melody's manager took was delighted with her achievement, but he also said how much fun it was to manage her for the six months she was working toward her trip.

If you have salespeople whose production is consistently inconsistent—too many peaks and valleys—then your best chance to change this is to help get them excited about and committed to their own goals. I've seen this process smooth out the ups and downs as salespeople become dedicated to their own growth for their own reasons.

One additional note about point #11, the support group: In the early 1990s I was conducting a goals program in mid-November, and I suggested that my clients bring their families. A seven-year-old girl named Emily had great fun cutting out pictures of things she wanted and taping them to her poster board. When it came time for "show and tell," she volunteered to come up to the front of the room and speak to the group, numbering almost 100 people. Her number one goal was to get a kitten. Immediately after she mentioned it, somebody from the back of the room shouted, "You've got one!"

Shocked, she looked up with a questioning look on her face. The voice in the back continued, "Our cat just had kittens. You can have your choice of any from the litter." Emily was so delighted she quickly rushed through the rest of her goals. A supporting cast can make success happen quickly.

If your salespeople aren't as committed as they need to be, isn't it time to take goal-setting for a test drive? It's the best chance you have to help the Tamaras of the world avoid the valleys in her performance.

☞ Key Thoughts

❖ Being committed to clear, realistic goals puts you on the right path and keeps you there.

❖ If you don't track it, you don't do it. Neither will your sales people.

❖ Not having goals is like driving to an unknown destination without a map. And gas prices are going up!

❖ Goals are about the future. Forget the past; it's over. That's why they call it past!

If You Sell

If your manager isn't excited about goal-setting, you can certainly use it for yourself. Why not you approach your manager with the following:

❖ A short list of things you are committed to obtaining in the next 12 months

❖ The reasons in writing why they're important to you

❖ What they're going to cost you

❖ A plan for achieving them

❖ A request for him to be your coach and cheerleader through the process

He's going to get excited about helping you. Even if you're lacking an effective plan, your manager will help you develop one. If this isn't the case, it's probably time for you to look for a new manager. Unless, of course, your company is also looking for a new manager. And by the way, you may be what they're looking for!

So this is what the big picture of motivation looks like. What about the shorter time frames?

Contests and Incentives

Most managers use contests and incentive programs to "get people motivated." In light of the previous chapter I it's time to reconsider how they work—and why they don't. If:

❖ the same two or three salespeople are always competing at the end of the contest period for the prize,

❖ halfway through some of your salespeople have given up because they have no chance of winning,

❖ the rewards and prizes don't generate excitement among your sales staff, and

❖ you don't see the expected bump in sales activity and results during the contest period,

then it's time to reassess.

Effective contests can be motivating to everyone if:

❖ everyone can win (note that I didn't say that everyone has the same chance of winning),

❖ the rewards are relevant, and

❖ people actually know how they can win.

You achieve these objectives by customizing every contest to fit your group. Your overall goal is an increase in an activity or result. Why not structure your program so that you measure each person's increase and reward accordingly? It might go something like this:

You want an increase in sales from new customers, because that's where your growth in revenue and market share must come from.

1. If in a typical quarter each of your salespeople opens one or two new accounts, you can consider that to be your base line.

2. Every salesperson will get a C-level award/bonus/prize for closing an order from a new account starting with the third new account.

3. Starting with the fifth new account, add a B-level award. With the eighth new account, add an A-level award. Each new level of award/bonus/prize is worth more.

4. Whoever lands the most new accounts wins the grand prize.

5. A second grand prize (not quite as valuable) goes to the salesperson who has the greatest increase over his historical average of new account acquisition.

6. What are the prizes? You can use catalogs (Saks, Bloomingdale's, L. L. Bean, REI, Best Buy, etc.) and categorize the prizes by dollar levels. Of course you'll make the rewards fit the increased revenue levels so both the sales staff and the company wins. Do you see how this ensures participants won't grumble about prizes not being relevant to

them? A grand prize like a trip can be selected from travel agency brochures you provide. Another reason I like catalogs is that the pictures and descriptions are created to hook your Child with their fantasy-like images and verbiage. Isn't advertising wonderful?

Part II

Sales Psychology

Chapter 11

The Psychology of Selling

Orchestrating Client Interactions

Most of us weren't born as salespeople. I personally got into sales as a temporary place to hang my hat. I had just finished several enjoyable (but financially unrewarding) years of classroom teaching, and considered my first sales job as something to do until I discovered my true calling. It seemed only natural to sell something I was familiar with, but that presented a problem for me in 1977. I knew almost nothing about the business world, even less about things like computers (the "future," I was told) and the software that ran them. So I took a job selling education for DeVry Tech in Atlanta. My sales manager (she was called "the director of admissions" for public relations reasons) Marge was exceptionally skilled at teaching me how to present our school and the degree programs we offered. She sent me to a one-day sales program taught by one of the popular sales trainers, and he dazzled me not only with his ability to sell anything but also with his fearlessness.

My own experience in selling, however, wasn't so dazzling. I memorized words and phrases, even pregnant pauses after I asked certain tie-down or closing questions, but my prospects weren't impressed. Neither was my manager.

It wasn't until my next sales job as an executive recruiter that I learned what was missing. The small recruiting firm that hired me was unusual because it was owned and managed by two guys who had graduate degrees in clinical psychology. They believed that to sell effectively, you have to understand the people you're selling to. This made a lot of sense to me. When I was in graduate school one of my professors used to tell us, "You don't teach reading; you don't teach history; you don't teach math. You teach kids! Focus on them!"

Similarly, the common denominator of selling is the people you're selling to. I enrolled in numerous sales training courses and programs—some were excellent, some mediocre, and some almost insulting in their antiquated approaches. Although I learned from all of them, I learned much more about selling from studying people...the prospects who bought and those who didn't. And why. Always why—why they did this, why they didn't do that, and why I was surprised by what happened. And in the early days of my sales career, I was surprised frequently.

What follows is a list of the most important insights I learned, which enabled me to sell more successfully. Your salespeople might also find them helpful:

❖ People always bought for their reasons—not necessarily mine.

❖ Whenever I didn't understand why and how they bought, I missed key information, which undermined my selling effort.

❖ Why they needed what I was selling—or why they didn't need it—was more important than anything I had to tell or show them.

❖ Every time a prospect bought, it was because of a gap—real or perceived—between where he was and where he wanted to be. This gap was more than just an intellectual need. The prospect usually felt the impact of this gap, emotionally and personally.

❖ My prospect saw and felt this gap as a challenge, a problem, or an opportunity, depending on his situation at the time.

❖ Whenever my prospect didn't perceive a gap, he rarely bought anything.

Statistically, it's unlikely that many of you reading these words are Buddhist. More than 2,500 years ago the Buddha spoke of the "eight worldly winds." He described eight experiences (four pairs, actually) that blow our lives back and forth, as a wind blows a leaf. They are:

1.		2.
Pleasure	and	Pain
Gain	and	Loss
Praise	and	Blame
Fame	and	Shame

He explained that with the exception of those few enlightened individuals who were unshakably grounded in the Absolute (nirvana), life consisted of chasing the experiences in column 1 and running away from those in column 2. You don't have to be a practicing Buddhist to appreciate how relevant this view is today.

Let's consider these four pairs as motivators in the buying process. Obviously, the words in the first column describe OK feelings, a basic human objective. The second column represents not-OK feelings, which we're all trying to avoid. The things that motivate us haven't changed much over

2,500 years. It's reasonable to assume that if we want to persuade or sell anything to anybody, we might want to consider these eight worldly winds in our approach. They form the reasons why people buy.

At the recruiting firm where I worked, I had the opportunity to train Amy, a newly hired salesperson. I told her, "Amy, you're going to learn how to present our firm in a good light, and what to do when people give you objections, and all that. But first—and most important—let's spend some time on why people would want to work with us."

And then I began to talk about the gaps that both companies (who pay our fees) and individuals (who we recruit) are experiencing. Companies were looking to gain production from a new employee and avoid a loss of production from the vacancy created when the previous worker left.

The candidates we were trying to recruit may have been looking to gain more money, better working conditions or more pleasure from working with a better team or in a more challenging job. Some were trying to avoid certain situations—perhaps the shame of being associated with a firm that deserved its bad reputation, the loss of income due to having lost market share, the blame associated with a program that failed, and so on.

Individuals or companies interested in working with us saw a gap they wanted to narrow or close. Sometimes they perceived it as an opportunity for gain, but just as often they were moving away from (what they perceived as) a losing situation. In every instance, their motivation—why they were receptive to our help—was critical to establishing our value as a provider of service.

Do you have salespeople skilled at presenting your capabilities, but who aren't as competent in uncovering the gaps clients must experience before they care about those capabilities? They aren't your top performers, and they won't be until they learn how to focus on what drives any successful selling experience—why a prospect might need/want to work with you.

Let's consider some other industries. For example, if you work in financial services, then your prospects might be experiencing a gap between where they are and where they'd like to be, with respect to:

❖ Having enough money to retire at a certain age

❖ Having a solid savings plan in place that will enable their kids to attend college without going into debt

❖ Reducing their tax liability

❖ Getting the kind of attention they want from their current advisor

❖ Receiving timely advice from an advisor who truly understands their goals and concerns

If you sell advertising, then your prospects might be experiencing a gap related to:

❖ Targeting a particular demographic

❖ The amount of traffic they're seeing in their stores

❖ The name brand recognition they enjoy

❖ Growing or defending their share of market

❖ The perception in the market of their value or image

❖ The acceptance of a new or improved product in the market

❖ The expectations they had about what advertising was going to provide them

If you sell scanning hardware and software systems, then your prospects might have gaps in:

❖ The ability to scan large documents without losing time or quality

❖ The ability to locate and share documents quickly in a large network

❖ Capabilities of sharing data in multiple formats across a wide area network

If you sell accounting services, then a good prospect might have gaps related to:

❖ Being able to plan effectively in order to minimize tax liabilities

❖ Decision-making capabilities having complex financial implications in a business

❖ Ensuring their firm is in compliance in an highly regulatory environment

❖ Feeling secure that in the event of an IRS audit they won't be vulnerable

If you sell environmental impact consulting services, qualified prospects could have gaps in:

❖ Understanding the financial liability different decisions might incur

❖ Knowing how to anticipate and manage effectively public reaction to business decisions

❖ Understanding where to invest time and resources to influence particular environmental legislation

Every company in every industry is challenged with gaps they want to narrow or close. It's the job of your sales staff to employ appropriate selling skills to conduct profound discussions about those gaps and their impact with their clients. Note that nowhere in the previous sentence did I mention your solutions. Client gaps must come before your solutions.

What Is a Salesperson's Job?

Every salesperson believes in the motto, *We solve problems.*

Consider how your salespeople apportion their time when they're in front of prospects and clients—when they're selling.

Years ago I established a sales training program for a leading software company, taking it to a dozen or more offices around the country. Most of their sales staff were highly technical people—they lived in their Adult. At one office the sales team proudly informed me that they took the first 5 to 10 minutes of every new client meeting to tell them about their company history and how the software was developed.

"That's a terrific strategy," I said. "What percentage of new clients are waiting eagerly to hear that information when you first meet them?" After pondering the question, they all agreed that something less than 2 percent of their clients wanted that approach.

They clearly focused on the first word of the motto: *We* solve problems.

Most salespeople apportion the largest percentage of their time on the Solve. After all, they tell me, this is the consultative approach, and it establishes credibility and can win sales.

Well—perhaps. But only after you know what the problems are, and after your client has demonstrated convincingly why he's committed to solving them. In other words, the gap has to deeply experienced—felt—for the client in order for your solution to have maximum impact.

In every company where I've trained or consulted, the top performers are those who have developed the expertise in identifying gaps and the impact they have on their clients. Interestingly, they aren't always the most technically knowledgeable about all the bits and bytes of their products. Of course they know how to talk intelligently about what they're selling. But their true expertise centers on the people they're selling to and the problems they're facing.

As you develop and refine your sales strategy you'll want to consider the following questions with your staff:

❖ Why do clients buy from us?

❖ What are the gaps that we help our clients narrow or close?

❖ How do we uncover them on a sales call?

❖ What questions must we ask and get answered on every sales call before we start "selling" our services?

❖ How receptive are our prospects to answering these questions?

❖ Do we tend to get only short answers to these questions, or do we enter into a dialog where we learn more about their situation?

❖ Once we uncover these gaps, how do we get our prospects to tell us about their impact on their company? On them personally?

❖ What percentage of time in an average sales call is spent on "problem" or "gap" that the prospect is experiencing?

❖ What percentage of time in an average sales call is spent on our presentation of a solution to these gaps?

Of course, you'll want to role-play these scenarios with

your salespeople so you can see and hear how well prepared they really are. If any of your salespeople find themselves doing most of the talking on their sales calls, they aren't exploring the gaps, and the prospects aren't involved enough.

☞ Key Thought

❖ Educating clients should first be about the gaps they are facing. This will help distinguish you from your competition. There will be time later to educate about your company, your service, yourself.

Questions

I'm sure you teach questioning tactics to your salespeople. Some of them are more skilled than others, and their questions yield better results. Returning to our ego states model, we can see below how questions play out in the transactions:

Effective questions from salesperson   Prospect

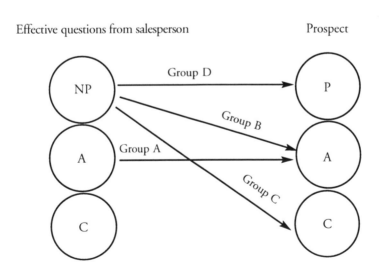

Don't be put off by how complicated this looks! Your best

salespeople are already doing this; they just aren't thinking about it too much.

Group A Questions and Statements

Adult to Adult; getting facts and data about the gaps, explaining how you help clients address specific problems.

❖ What's the biggest challenge you're currently facing?

❖ Where is your biggest opportunity to grow?

❖ Who is responsible for…?

❖ There are two ways we can configure a system to meet your needs

❖ We have been ranked in the top five in the industry for customer service for the past four years.

Group B Questions

From the salesperson's Nurturing Parent to the client's Adult. These tend to be open-ended questions that lead to dialogs. They are generally follow up questions from responses to Group A inquiries.

❖ Can you help me understand just how that affects your department?

❖ Tell me, what impact would a more streamlined system have on your profitability in the out years?

❖ Can you share with me how the ideal solution would have to be configured to meet your spatial requirements?

❖ If this process isn't in place by the end of the first quarter, how will that affect your department?

❖ If there was one area where your current supplier could improve, what would that be?

❖ What constraints pose the greatest challenges to you getting the exact solution you would like to have?

Group C Questions

From the salesperson's Nurturing Parent to the client's Child:

❖ Assuming we could implement these changes, how would you benefit?

❖ What would it mean to you if we could meet your accelerated deadline?

❖ It certainly sounds like an ambitious target. What happens if you don't reach it?

❖ If you did hit that goal, how would that affect you?

❖ How did you feel when they didn't meet your deadline last month?

Group D Questions

From the salesperson's Parent to the client's Parent:

❖ If opting for a less expensive system would increase the chances for downtime down the road, would you still want to consider it?

❖ If you had to choose between staying within your projected budget and implementing the entire system to generate cost savings in the ensuing years, which would make more sense?

❖ From your experience in the industry, which view is more congruent with your company's values?

❖ How do you think top management will view this situation?

We can quibble about whether a particular question involves more of the client's Child, Adult, or Parent, but that's not the point here. Good questioning strategies uncover the client's values, which involve his wants, thinks, fears, and shoulds.

There are powerful psychological advantages to asking

questions with your Nurturing Parent instead of your Adult. First, your client doesn't feel cross-examined or under attack, which forces him into his Child. If he feels that your questions are too abrupt or intrusive, he feels not-OK and resents you for it. Whenever a salesperson's questions sound harsh or confrontational, your client will shut down or go on the attack. You have become the enemy—not the way to win business.

The more common—and less effective—approach to questions and statements is shown in the diagram below:

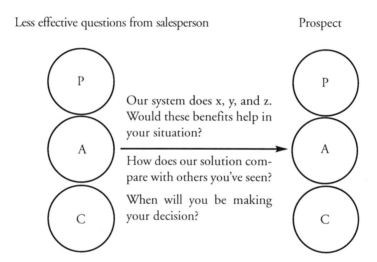

Less effective questions from salesperson   Prospect

P

A
Our system does x, y, and z. Would these benefits help in your situation?

How does our solution compare with others you've seen?

When will you be making your decision?

C

P

A

C

These kinds of questions seek to uncover essential information, but they don't engage all of the prospect's ego states, and this means you're unlikely to generate any meaningful dialog or conversation. You've witnessed these calls too often—the salesperson does most of the talking, centered on the value he's offering, while the prospect sits with arms crossed and mouth closed. The salesperson gets only perfunctory answers to his questions, learning little. By the meeting's end, the salesperson may know what the client is interested in (but not why). He also fails to learn what gaps he's confronted with or how he feels about them. This approach doesn't uncover these essential issues that move clients to take decisive action.

If You Sell

❖ If you're not developing a dialog with your client, you'll be stuck giving a monologue. Very few people make a living at monologues, and in your current job you won't be one of them.

❖ List the questions you typically ask on your sales calls. How many of them get your client talking? Use the previous pages to create a more balanced mix of questions and then practice, practice, practice.

Client Expectations

In the financial services industry the typical sales cycle involves two meetings. At the first, the financial advisor asks lots of questions—some companies use a standard questionnaire, called a financial needs analysis (FNA). At the second meeting, solutions are presented and discussed, and the advisor attempts to close the sale. In the 1980s I was training life insurance agents for a major company, and at a regional meeting one young lady asked me for some advice about how to get her prospect to buy. "Tomorrow evening is the closing appointment," she said. Wondering aloud, I asked her, "Does the prospect know it's a closing appointment?" There was silence in the room, and then a few smiles of recognition and then, "Aha!"

We make it hard on ourselves—and on our clients—if we neglect to establish clear expectations in advance of every meeting. How can you meet a client's expectations if you don't know what they are? And who really wants a fight when showing up for a closing appointment?

I've never met a company that didn't want to meet or exceed client expectations. But I'm amazed at how few firms have a strategy in place to identify precisely what these expectations are. It's no wonder that so many clients grumble about dissatisfaction. If this strategy isn't an integral part of your selling approach, you are gambling, and the odds are against your success. If you've been around professional selling for more than a few years, you've encountered your share of selling systems. I want to share with you the most effective selling system on the market today! Are you ready?

The Best Sales Strategy Ever!

1. Identify what your client

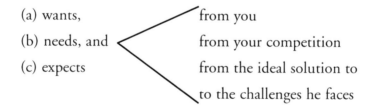

(a) wants,
(b) needs, and
(c) expects

from you
from your competition
from the ideal solution to
to the challenges he faces

2. Identify the why behind the what—why he wants and needs and expects these things.

3. If your client's expectations aren't realistic, help him understand this and then help him readjust his expectations.

4. If you can, give your client what he wants and needs within the scope of his expectations.

5. Return to step #1 and repeat.

Too obvious? Too simplistic? Will this strategy benefit your clients? Will it benefit your salespeople? Will it create a win-win relationship? How many on your sales team skillfully employ these five steps on a daily basis? Those who do know the following:

❖ Where they are and where they need to go next

❖ How to get there

❖ If they can get there

❖ What their chances of success are

❖ When to give up

❖ How best to invest their time and energy

❖ How best to plan and prioritize their time

❖ How to deliver on their sales forecasts

❖ How to meet and exceed their clients expectations

❖ How to meet and exceed the expectations you have

And the rest of your salespeople? Remember—hope is not a strategy!

What does your next client expect from you?

❖ A dog-and-pony show, followed by a quick exit?

❖ The same old song-and-dance that he gets from all of your competitors?

❖ A defense of your service? Of your pricing? Of your support? Of your solution? Of your installation?

❖ A list of references so he can lower his perceived risk?

❖ An explanation about why nobody in the industry seems able to solve his problems?

❖ An outlet where he can vent his frustrations?

❖ Your view on why his last supplier couldn't meet

his expectations?

* ❖ Advice on how to make a critical buying decision?

* ❖ Advice on how best to reconfigure a complex solution?

* ❖ Help with an internal selling challenge so he (and you) can solve his problems and narrow his gaps?

* ❖ The moon?

You may not know, but isn't it your primary objective to identify what your client expects so you can determine if and how you can deliver? Or whether you even want to try? Can you think of anything more pivotal to a business relationship than client expectations? This strategy is just part of an overall focus on the client before zeroing in on what you're selling. Your best salespeople don't just identify client expectations well. They also negotiate and manage client expectations to a realistic level.

Your salespeople can be divided into two groups:

1. Weaker

2. Stronger

Regardless of what criteria you use, you'll find that your weaker group allows their clients and prospects to have unrealistically high expectations, while the stronger group manages client expectations down to a level where they can meet and exceed them. Naturally need for approval, fear of rejection, and discomfort with hearing No! all help determine who fits into which group. Too often when you debrief your weaker salespeople you'll find that they rarely uncover their client's expectations until it's too late to do anything about them. They're afraid to hear bad news—they want to avoid feeling not-OK—so they frequently don't even think to ask. Remember the growth continuum?—They stop short for fear of going too far.

As you emphasize this essential step in your sales cycle—with explanations, role-playing and debriefing—many of your weaker salespeople will begin to take more control of the entire sales process. As for those who don't, they aren't going to grow enough to become successful.

How should your salespeople respond when they realize that their clients' expectations are unrealistically high? As we'll see in the next chapter, people (and corporate cultures) have different values. If your client is expecting to get Saks Fifth Avenue quality for a K-Mart price, it's your job

❖ to uncover why he has such expectations,

❖ to help him adjust his expectations so he's not disappointed later on, or perhaps

❖ to help him understand how to help others in his organization to readjust their own expectations downward.

This conversation is where your people establish your value in the client's mind. It's here that you discuss how realistic his requirements are, and whether or not anyone can meet them. It's where you lead your client to confirm that he will get what he pays for. It's here where you establish your credibility as an authoritative source. And it's here that many sales are made—or lost.

Finally, compare the profit margins on the sales where client expectations were identified early on and managed well with those sales where this did not occur. It's often the key to shrinking profit margins.

☞ Key Thoughts

❖ Satisfied clients and acceptable profit margins meet at the point where realistic expectations are established.

❖ Weak salespeople end up fighting unrealistically high client expectations, creating trouble for all parties involved.

❖ A large part of any company's success is determined by its ability to understand, manage, meet, and exceed market expectations. This process must be part of your selling strategy.

If You Sell

❖ Review your client meetings for the past two months, or whatever time period you need to collect a large enough sample. Consider the following:

—Each client's or prospect's expectations of you and your company

—When you uncovered these expectations

—How well you met or exceeded them

—How you responded if these expectations were unrealistic

—Did you address this fact or did you wimp out, creating problems of unmet expectations or lower profits down the road?

❖ If you aren't measuring up here, get with your manager and develop a corrective action plan. This will improve your results dramatically!

Chapter 12

The Psychology of Buying

Your Client's Mindset

It's not really possible to separate the buying and selling processes because they are so interdependent and overlapping. Nevertheless, we need to understand what takes place in the mind of the buyer in order to have an outstanding career in sales or sales management.

Consider a typical corporate history below:

Past	Past	Past	Past	Present
#1	#2	#3	#4	#5
Symptoms of gaps/ problems	Cost/Cause discussions	Decision to investigate solutions	Decision to solve problem	Today's sales call

1. At this point in time, the prospective buyer notices symptoms of a gap, often a problem. These symptoms can

include things like a drop in revenues or profits, missed delivery deadlines, inadequate or late information that affects critical decision-making, missed opportunities to gain market share, increased customer complaints, increasing quality defects, loss of market share, lost clients, and so forth. Each industry and company lives in its own world of gaps, problems, and challenges.

2. The prospective buyer holds discussions to assess the cost of the gaps and their causes. In some companies this can take months (or even years).

3. Here a decision is made, often based on what the gaps are costing the company, to "see what's out there." The prospective buyer is looking for an education, but he may not be serious yet.

4. Based on the continued or even worsening gaps and accompanying costs, the prospective buyer becomes a serious buyer. This prospect usually has a deadline (often unrealistic because of how they make decisions) for having a solution in place. Note that some companies arrive at this step by changing top management or corporate strategy. Companies can also move backwards from this step—all the way back to step #1, from a similar change in management or strategy.

5. Salesperson meets with the buyer/prospect/client.

Unfortunately, most salespeople at step #5 discuss only the present and the future—what the requirements are and what the solution and its benefits might look like. Skilled sales professionals use much of this meeting to investigate what happened in steps 1 through 4. From this they learn vital information, including the following:

❖ What the real gaps are

❖ How they're perceived and felt, and by whom

❖ The impact they're having on the company/individual

❖ How they arrived at a decision to address the situation and close the gap

❖ What solutions they've already seen and considered

❖ What they liked and disliked about those solutions

❖ When a buying decision will be made

❖ If a buying decision will be made

❖ What are the chances of winning this business

❖ And much more

Your most successful salespeople think and question strategically to elicit the information they need. Once again, this strategy is conducted from their Adult and their Nurturing Parent, not their Child. For them selling is an intellectual experience rather than emotional.

And what about your less successful salespeople? Instead of uncovering this vital information, don't they assume and guess about it? Your least successful salespeople probably aren't even aware that such a strategy exists.

If You Sell

The client's past is the basis for their present and the future. If you don't understand what happened in the past, and why, you're not prepared to move into the future successfully.

For most prospects their Parent, Adult, and Child ego states are all involved in the buying process. This holds true in corporate as well as in personal buying decisions. From a TA perspective, let's consider what we want to happen.

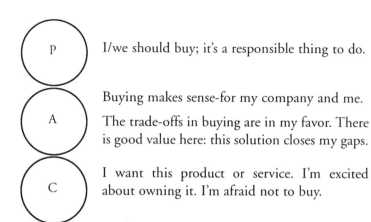

P — I/we should buy; it's a responsible thing to do.

A — Buying makes sense-for my company and me.
The trade-offs in buying are in my favor. There is good value here: this solution closes my gaps.

C — I want this product or service. I'm excited about owning it. I'm afraid not to buy.

In most buying processes requiring a significant investment, all three ego states get involved.

Around 1980, I was in the market for a new car. I enjoy shopping for a new car, and I really liked Volvo's new model, the 760 Turbo. On the test drive I found the acceleration to be surprisingly quick and the interior luxurious. Back then, owning a Volvo announced that you were intelligent and didn't follow the pack. The car represented good value for those who weren't afraid to "go their own way."

After figuring out how I could negotiate the best price (somewhere around $20,000), I went through a process that makes me laugh today. I went to a newsstand and bought various car magazines, searching through the ratings until I found one that gave the Volvo 760 Turbo the highest rating.

What was this process I went through?

❖ My Child fell in love with the car.

❖ My Adult figured out that it represented good value and a good purchase.

❖ I then did enough research to convince (my Little Professor was probably at work here) my Parent to give the rest of me permission to buy what I wanted.

Unfortunately for both buyer and seller, far too often what happens in a buyer/seller situation can be diagrammed below:

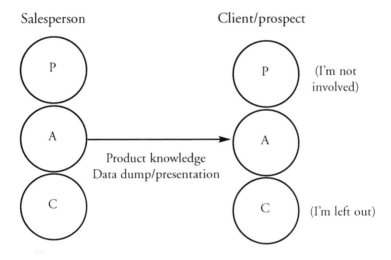

Salesperson   Client/prospect

P

P   (I'm not
          involved)

A   Product knowledge   A
         Data dump/presentation

C   C   (I'm left out)

Traditional selling sequence:

1. Salesperson asks a few questions and uncovers facts, data, and information.

2. Salesperson immediately proceeds from his Adult to explain and present a solution (remember We Solve Problems?) including additional and extraneous information in hopes of establishing credibility and "building a case." This step can come from the Child's need for approval and fear of asking too many questions, just as much as from an Adult selling strategy.

3. Client/prospect is engaged intellectually (Adult) but not emotionally (Child) and is often left on his own to

understand how this buying decision is the responsible thing to do (Parent). With little emotional involvement, there's no opportunity for the buyer's Child to convince his Parent to rationalize the purchase.

4. When only the Buyer's Adult is engaged, is it any wonder why he so often needs more time to make his decision? The Adult is the part of the personality that evaluates, discriminates and thinks it over. When it's the only ego state "in play," the decision will be extended as the buyer digests and continues to evaluate the facts.

5. Even worse, during this gestation period your competitors will visit the Buyer. One of them employs her skill to get the client's Child and Parent ego states involved, and as a result, he buys her solution, sometimes even when it's inferior to yours. We have a technical term for this process—it's called *getting outsold!*

More Questions About Your Salespeople

With respect to all of your salespeople: How interactive are their sales calls?

Are they more of a monolog or a dialog? (Very few people in America make a living from monologs.) Many salespeople, lacking either effective sales technique or guts to use it, won't have much of an answer.

Locate your salespeople on this continuum:

Monolog: Salesperson talks   Dialog: 50/50 split
80+ percent of the time

Your top salespeople are probably on the right side of the continuum. Dialogs are part of their everyday sales approach.

Exercise

Score each of your salespeople as follows: 1 = a definite weakness; 2 = acceptable, but still needs improvement; and 3 = a definite strength.

_____ Client meetings are more interactive instead of one-sided presentations.

_____ Comes away with more vital information about the client's buying strategies and values than the average salesperson.

_____ Clients see him more as a partner in the buying process than a vendor who's selling a commodity.

_____ He is surprised less often than other salespeople by how things turn out.

_____ His forecasts are more accurate and require fewer revisions and explanations (and excuses).

Take a look at which of your salespeople produce higher revenues and profits—for the most part, aren't they the ones with the highest scores here? These individuals have developed the "people skills" that enable them to orchestrate interactive client meetings instead of just talking features and benefits. They're able to get their clients' Parent, Adult, and Child to interact as well.

Let's take a closer look at how they accomplish this. One way is to understand each client's values. Further, you must help the client understand the consequences of his values. This can apply to both individual and corporate values.

Below is what I call the values triangle.

Naturally, every client wants the best of all possible worlds, meaning all three points on the triangle. This goal isn't achievable very often in a free market economy. In reality, many people aren't willing or able to pay for the best, and many willingly sacrifice quality or service in order to save money. After all, not everyone who needs transportation buys an S600 Mercedes. Most people realize that the best quality comes with a high price tag. In other words, you pay for what you get, and you get what you pay for.

An effective sales strategy that every salesperson can adopt is to identify where a particular client's values lie. If you asked a client to place an X inside this triangle where these three values meet for her or her company, you'll get a quick reference point about your chances of doing business.

It's also essential that you, as a company, understand where you are on this triangle. If you offer solutions based on outstanding quality (it could be the best overall solution, most whistles and bells, expert advice, etc.), then you'd be located toward the lower left point.

Consider for a moment if where your company—or a particular product or service you sell—is located on the triangle, and where your prospects are. Do you have a good match? Are you calling on the right accounts? Conversely, are your prospects buying what you're selling?

Thousands of sales calls each day in America are unproductive due to this poor fit—buying values and selling values are too far apart. Remember those sales opportunities when you tried to bend and stretch your own values to fit the client's demands, and still didn't make the sale? Or even worse, remember when you did get the sale, and later wished you hadn't? Trouble accounts are often based on values not in alignment. And painful experience has taught you that just because you win a sale doesn't mean you have a good fit. As we discussed in the previous chapter, client expectations can't always be met profitably. Use your corporate strategy to determine how far you can and should go with each client.

On my own sales calls I've actually drawn this triangle and asked my prospect to determine where he saw his company. It can streamline your sales cycle and is usually the start of a revealing discussion. After all, if your prospect's values make it unlikely that he'll buy what you're selling, isn't the best time to find out right now?

What do you do when your prospect's value is toward the top (lowest price) and your strengths are at the two bottom points? Don't argue or debate! It's time for an open discussion about any gaps he may be experiencing or trying to avoid. Ask about opportunities he may be missing. Ask about instances where he ended up unhappy when he bought the lowest price.

A more likely circumstance is when a prospect tells you that all three values are important to him, even equally important. Don't accept this statement. Ask about which one he'd sacrifice if he had to make a choice—and aren't buyers faced with this choice every day? Salespeople who are afraid to confront tough situations won't bring up the unavoidable fact that buyers don't receive top quality and service when paying the lowest price. Something has to give. The closer you get to quality and service, the farther away you travel from lowest price. Similarly, the closer you get to lowest price, the farther you are from best quality and best service.

It's the responsibility of your salespeople to make sure their prospects and clients are educated about what they will give up with each choice. And it's your responsibility to make sure your people have the skills to do this. You know you've achieved a key objective when your prospect tells you, "I guess you get what you pay for." Note that this is quite different from you telling your client, "You get what you pay for." Words from a salesperson are often taken as a sales pitch, and are discounted. If these same words come from your client, they have credibility.

☞ Key Thought\If You Sell

❖ In terms of values, is your prospect in the market for what you're selling? If you don't know, you're likely wasting valuable time.

The Why and the What

A second way in which top salespeople demonstrate more control in their client meetings is by uncovering the "why" behind the "what." How often have you met with a new salesperson—or even a veteran who's not a strong producer—and heard, "Here's what the client is going to do: _____"? You ask, "Why is the client going to do that? or "How do you know?" What follows are guesses, assumptions, mind reading, and hopes.

☞ Key Thought

❖ The *why* always drives the *what*.

How many of your salespeople have this key thought in mind when planning their questions on a sales call? Certainly your best ones. What keeps the others from asking the "why" questions? Let us recount the ways:

❖ Need for approval

❖ Fear of rejection

❖ Fear of being too aggressive

❖ Fear of making waves

To summarize, stuck in the Child, they stop short for fear of going too far. These fears and needs come from the Adaptive Child, which should be quite familiar to you by now.

If You Sell

❖ If you don't know where your prospects and clients are on the values triangle, it's time to find out. Practice by role-playing these questions with your colleagues until it becomes second nature.

❖ How much mind reading are you doing about why people do what they do? Here's another opportunity to role-play asking why when a client tells you what—what she's going to do, what she has to have, what she wants you to do next.

❖ As you become comfortable and skilled at getting the key information from these two exercises, you'll find selling much more enjoyable and profitable.

Let's return to the buyers-prospects and clients. What do you think is their main complaint about salespeople? Here is a common list:

- ❖ They don't know their product well enough.
- ❖ They talk too much.
- ❖ They don't understand my business or my concerns
- ❖ They are too pushy.

We can extend the list indefinitely, but it seems to me that everything listed above can be distilled to one major complaint about salespeople: They are all alike! Maybe you don't hear it in these words, but isn't that the essence of the other complaints? Doesn't everything reduce to this one fundamental issue? When this occurs, the buyer is often treats your product or service as a commodity, and ends up going with the lowest price.

Now consider the response a salesperson would get who instead

- ❖ conducted a thorough discussion about important gaps between where the client was and wanted to be;
- ❖ asked insightful questions and was sincerely interested in the answers;
- ❖ was more interested in listening and learning than in talking;
- ❖ uncovered the client's personal and company values;
- ❖ had a good understanding why the client believed what he believed; and
- ❖ had the guts to offer solid, candid advice—even if it meant telling a client where he was going wrong and why.

Salespeople who operate this way succeed. Those who are learning how to operate this way are growing and becoming successful. Those who don't fall into either category become your headaches.

Buying Mistakes

Not every company—or individual, for that matter—has an effective strategy for making buying decisions and good purchases. I'm convinced that most don't. This can present real challenges and problems, but you can also view it as an opportunity. See it as an opportunity to:

❖ Establish credibility

❖ Solidify a relationship

❖ Gain a competitive advantage

❖ Diminish or shut out competition

❖ Plant seeds in your prospect's mind

❖ And help your prospect avoid costly mistakes

What costly mistakes? Make a list of them. They are the most common and costly mistakes that buyers of your solutions tend to make, and later regret. We came up with the following list of buyer mistakes for Browning Pools, a quality builder of in-ground swimming pools on the East Coast:

❖ Not having your pool company conduct a thorough analysis of the landscape to identify potential drainage problems that could render a new swimming pool unusable

❖ Not understanding the importance of having year-round access to a full-time service department

❖ Accepting a simple drawing instead requiring a design that integrates pool, patios, decks, landscaping, and buildings

❖ Not having a clear understanding of the strengths and weaknesses of each category of pool liners

❖ Not getting a first-hand look at several installed pools from each pool company they are considering

❖ Not getting a complete estimate of all costs involved in the entire project from each company

These are all valid considerations. They also play to my client's strengths. Browning is known for their top quality pools, their excellent service, and their integrity in everything they do. They help their customers become knowledgeable by conducting Saturday morning caravan tours of pools they've built. Buyers get a free education about how to get the pool they really want, while learning how to avoid all the mistakes we listed above. Customers love these tours, which shorten the selling and buying cycles. Browning's outstanding reputation and their large referral business are the envy of the industry.

The point here is that in your market there are mistakes that buyers make repeatedly, to their detriment as well as yours. If you sell at the Best Quality and Best Service points on the Values Triangle, you should be spending time educating your prospects on how to buy. The more you understand about the buyer's point of view, the more effective you can be with what you say to him.

Lowest Price

Best quality   **Best service/support**

Many companies have what I would call a standard or generic presentation that they go through on most initial sales calls. I don't believe this serves the company—or even the customer—well, because it assumes that all clients share the same values and want to learn the same things at the same point in time. But if your focus is on what the client wants and needs and why, your standard presentation won't always fit. Doesn't it make sense to find out before you give it?

I work with my clients to identify the typical buying mistakes their customers make. We then structure a win-win buying strategy around which they can educate their customers. If you want to engage your prospect, spend some time on the costly buying mistakes and how to avoid them. Within this discussion you will position your own strengths and strategies for helping clients close the gaps and problems they're facing. You may end up addressing many of the subjects contained in your generic presentation, but now they are related to your client's situation. Framing your key points and strengths in this way makes them memorable; generic presentations are quickly forgotten. Let your competitors present the old way, while you stand out. Provide your prospects with relevant, valuable information that establishes you as a credible authority, and you gain their trust and respect. And they become your clients.

Too many managers overlook this opportunity when preparing selling strategy. Make sure you don't.

Chapter 13

The Psychology of Prospecting

Looking for Gaps

When I started my sales training business in 1985, I was fortunate to land a nice account that provided me with a bit of regular income while I "learned the business." After I had delivered a couple of training classes for his sales team, my client, a general agent in the life insurance industry, asked me into his office for a chat. The first words out of his mouth were, "This is good stuff, Mark, but you know, every day we do business is a day closer to our relationship ending."

Talk about cold water thrown in your face! This was an instantaneous not-OK Child experience, but I was able to get back into my Adult and ask him what he meant. "It's simple," he replied. "All business relationships end sooner or later...after one year or 20 years, and for a variety of reasons. I preach this to my agents regularly, so they always know they have to be filling their pipeline. You can never stop prospecting if you want be successful and stay in business." If there's a more valuable business lesson, I've yet to hear it.

Notice that he didn't say you can never stop cold calling; it's prospecting that doesn't end.

For salespeople, this is where not-OK feelings surface most often and most painfully. They may originate from childhood messages about not talking to strangers or intruding on other people's time; they definitely deepen from your own prospecting experiences. The internal dialog running through the minds of most salespeople looks like this:

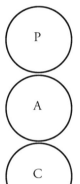

You have to prospect; it's part of your job. Don't be a wimp! (CP) You'll be OK. The last time wasn't so bad. (NP)

I can block out 45 minutes this morning to make some calls from my current list. I'll use that strategy we discussed in last week's sales meeting.

Maybe now's not a good day to cold call. Fridays work better. And my voice sounds a little scratchy today. What I really should do is work on those expense reports.

The Parent and Adult usually win, but sometimes not without a struggle and loss of valuable time. The Rebellious Child will procrastinate and come up all sorts of reasons not to cold call.

Cold calling, a subset of prospecting along with referrals, networking, direct mail marketing, and other activities, is where we need to focus, because this is where most salespeople encounter what they interpret as failure and rejection. Note that interpretations aren't always accurate; thus the word misinterpretation, which fits the scenario much better.

When I teach cold calling, I present salespeople with the following scenario: I have a cashier's check for $10,000 made out to you. There is only one reason I won't hand it to you right now. Remember the last cold call you received, either at work or at home? OK, now with respect to that call: I want you to tell me the name of the salesperson, the name of his company, and what he was selling. If you can accurately give me that information, you get the check. Now raise your hand if you are about to be $10,000 richer.

It's rare that a hand goes up. This leads to a discussion about how important and memorable most cold calls are in the minds of prospects. Do they really reject the other person? 95 percent of the time they don't remember enough about the conversation to have any opinion at all. Rejection is actually a misinterpretation of the event that just occurred. But it's also your choice to make—and to feel.

I've met many great cold callers over years, and I think these people are neurologically wired differently from most salespeople. Their combination of mindset, fearlessness and skills is rare and difficult to develop. Having said that, it's also true that most salespeople can improve their cold calling skills, and some can become masterful at it. However, there are some people who probably shouldn't be cold calling at all. Let's start by looking at who's not a likely candidate for success here so you can play the percentages when investing your time. Consider the following qualities:

1. Introverted

2. Afraid of rejection

3. High need for approval

4. Easily intimidated

5. Avoids high risk and uncertainty

6. Questionable self-esteem

7. Tendency to make excuses

8. Tendency to give up when the going gets tough

Right how you're probably thinking, *Why would anybody with even half of these qualities be in sales? I wouldn't hire somebody like that!*

Before you get too upset, take a couple of minutes to examine your salespeople and list those with at least three of these problems. There is no absolute rule here, but anyone with four or more will probably find it too painful to spend much time cold calling, and it's not going to be productive. Some salespeople will work hard enough on themselves to overcome these issues and stay out of their Child, but most will find it too difficult and painful. Square peg, round hole—don't force it.

Aside from the psychological baggage that salespeople start with, why is cold calling (both telephone and walking in) so difficult for so many? Part of the answer lies with the fact that the people they're calling are often busy and resent the interruption. Believing this can be enough to change a salesperson's mindset from determination to fear, moving him from his Adult to his Child. Furthermore, the typical cold call approach turns prospects off, because it

❖ sounds canned,

❖ sounds artificial,

❖ often insults our intelligence,

❖ sounds like every other cold call we get, and

❖ focuses on the salesperson instead of the prospect.

No wonder we feel "not-OK" when it's directed at us!

Let's recall two main points from the last chapter:

1. People want to narrow or close the gaps—for instance, between pleasure and pain, gain and loss.

2. People buy for their own reasons not necessarily those of the salesperson.

Any cold calling approach should be based on this understanding and should employ plenty of Nurturing Parent and sensitivity. Here's an approach we developed for financial advisors at a firm to target high-net-worth clients:

Sharon (financial advisor): George, I'm Sharon Baker with ABC Financial, and we work with clients who might be looking to inject an element of certainty to their retirement and other savings plans. Do you have just a minute or two so I can quickly explain the kinds of things I do, and then you can decide if it makes sense for us to talk?

George: OK, but I'm busy.

Sharon: I respect that and I'll be brief. Typically, when I speak with successful people they tell me they want solid investment advice geared to their own values and objectives…for retirement, funding education, or any other major life event. And of course, you may be looking for ways to reduce your tax burden as well. My clients also want an advisor who keeps them informed of changing opportunities, while not overwhelming them with too much detail. Let me ask you—do you think these ideas might be worth discussing?

Some subtle psychological points to consider here:

1. Sharon's opening lines are designed to catch George's attention.

2. She's polite and respectful, without sounding apologetic.

3. Her explanation of why she's calling highlights the most likely gaps that George is facing. She thereby implies a level of expertise about them, as well as potential solutions. She sounds authoritative.

4. Sharon ends her explanation with a nonthreatening question designed to open a conversation. You always have to open the discussion before you close the sale.

Sharon is neither aggressive nor wimpy. As a professional in her business, she is focused solely on identifying and helping clients solve problems. Her approach uses her Adult with some Nurturing Parent thrown in to soften her statements and questions.

Because Sharon knows that prospects on the phone generally reach an initial buying decision about whether this is worth their time in a matter of seconds, she has practiced her phrasing and voice until she's satisfied with how they sound. Having used her voicemail to record and refine her opening lines, Sharon is prepared to cold call with confidence. She blocks out time to prospect regularly by telephone, and she gets results.

☞ Key Thoughts

❖ If you don't know precisely how your voice will sound or what specific words you will use to open a cold call, you're not ready to make one.

❖ Don't use the point above as an excuse to avoid making cold calls! Your Parent and Adult ego states are in charge, not your Child. Prepare and go to work now!

I vividly remember an incident when I was just starting out as a sales trainer, in a city where I had no existing business and knew nobody. I was spending much of my time making walk-in cold calls on small businesses, attempting to sell training and coaching. Driving up Georgia Avenue in Silver Spring, Maryland, I saw a sign for an Allstate Insurance agency, so I pulled in the parking lot of the 10-story building where the agency was housed. I walked into the offices, and introduced myself to the administrative assistant, Sandi, telling her I wanted to speak to Steve, the agent. She smiled and said Steve was on the phone and would be off in a few minutes, offering me a seat. Here's what went through my head as I sat, waiting: *Steve will think I'm here to buy insurance. He won't be receptive to what I have to say. He probably already has training from his home office, and won't ever spend his own money to get sales help. He may even be outraged that I'm taking up his time to sell him. I'm going to look stupid, not just in front of him, but also in front of Sandi. This is going to be a disaster!*

With these thoughts running through my head, what do you think I did before Steve had finished his phone conversation? If you guessed that I got up and left without saying anything, give yourself a gold star. Below, I've diagrammed what happened:

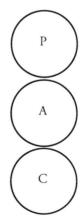

1. My Parent got me to walk in.

2. From my Adult came the request to speak to Steve.

3. While I waited, I fell into my Child, and that was the end of it.

4. As I walked to my car, my Parent screamed at me for wimping out. This continued as I started the engine and for several blocks as I drove away. Actually, this was healthy, because it forced me to reevaluate my long-term goals and daily objectives were. I was forced back into my Adult so I could understand what happened, how and why it happened, and resolve not to allow it to happen again.

Of course some people proceed to a step #5—they make excuses from their Child and sell them to their other ego states:

❖ That guy wasn't going to buy, so nothing was lost.

❖ I'll do better on the next one.

❖ This was only a warm up.

❖ Allstate agents are lousy prospects anyway.

As a manager, you've heard them all. As a salesperson, you may have thought them all. Perhaps you've both bought them all! But no longer.

For the first six months in my business, I tracked my activity level closely because I knew that level would determine how quickly I would start earning a good, consistent living. Along with my activity, I had a "psychological" goal to stay in my Adult and out of my Child on every sales call I made. Although I wasn't always successful, just having this objective kept my mind focused and my emotions on the shelf most of the time.

About five months into my sales training career, I had achieved some real success, although I was still doing some walk-in cold calling. One Friday morning I had just finished a training session for an employee benefits firm, and as I walked toward the elevator I saw a sign that read

Metropolitan Life Insurance, Capitol Region Office, with an arrow pointing around the corner. One of my prospecting rules was that whenever I was in an office building seeing clients, I had to make at least one walk-in cold call before leaving the building. So I headed toward the regional office. It was approaching noon, and people were streaming out for lunch or an early start to the weekend.

I strolled by the reception desk with no trouble, approached the vice-president's office, and knocked on the door. Fred Kutner, the vice president, looked up and saw that his administrative assistant had left for lunch. He smiled and waved me in.

I introduced myself as a sales trainer, but before I could go any further, he held up both hands, giving me the stop sign. He leaned forward in his chair, and said, "You know, I enjoy talking with sales trainers, and we've brought them in when they had something special for us. I have 15 offices in this region. Why don't you call my assistant Joan to schedule an appointment, and then you can tell me what you have."

Various thoughts and feelings came to mind, but then the realization hit me that at that moment I was standing 5 feet from Fred. Was I really going to drive back to my office and call his assistant Joan in hopes of getting an opportunity sometime in the future to get back within 5 feet of this guy?

In TA terms here's what was happening:

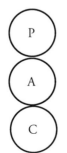

P — Don't give up! Don't wimp out!

A — How is going home and calling back later going to help me in this selling situation? What message will that send to Fred?

C — "Sure, Fred...anything you say."

My Child screamed at me, *Say "yes" and get out of here!*

My Adult told me this would be a poor strategy.

My Parent whispered, *You can do better than that! Hang in there!*

Here was my reply: "Fred, I can do that. You know—there are probably only a couple of reasons why we might want to talk. First of all, you may have a lot of agents spending huge amounts of time 'getting ready' to make cold calls, fearing rejection, and as a result they're not getting enough qualified appointments. Second, your agents probably have presented a ton of proposals to their prospects, but they can't figure out how to close them, or even who is still interested. Let me ask you—is either of these worth discussing?"

After a quick stare, Fred said, "Have a seat."

I looked at my watch. It was exactly 12 noon; we went to lunch at 1:20 p.m.. I had tapped into two painful gaps that were costing Fred's region millions of dollars in revenues, so naturally he had the time right then to talk with me...in this case, more than a hour. Fred became a valued client, and I worked with his 15 offices for several years.

☛ Key Thoughts

❖ When they are on the receiving end of a cold call, prospects want to know two things quickly: What is this about? Can this benefit (close any gaps for) me? The answers you provide enable them to decide whether or not to invest their time (either now or later).

❖ If you're in your Adult ego state, you have a chance to make something good happen. If you're in your Child, the odds are against you.

❖ If you can uncover gaps that are causing real problems, it's more likely that prospects will make the time to find out if you can help.

Direct Mail Prospecting

Most companies don't limit their prospecting efforts to just cold calling. Regardless of what else you're doing, focusing on the client gaps you narrow and close will increase your success. Consider direct mail.

Back in the 1980s, I was consulting with a small company that restored stained glass in churches in the eastern United States. The company president was ready to interview advertising agencies because he wanted a new brochure. I suggested that we first spend an hour to refine his objectives, and perhaps he might find a new brochure wasn't even necessary.

Together we made a list of all the reasons why a church would need and want to restore their stained glass. Here's what we came up with:

1. Outside air comes into the church

2. Moisture can cause damage

3. Windows look shabby

4. Extra heating costs resulting from leaks

5. Windows shake and rattle (but not roll)

From there, we developed this one-page letter.

Dear _____:

Do you find that:

❖ Congregation members sitting on the outside aisle complain of drafts in cold months?

❖ Your windowsills and frames are beginning to wear down?

❖ Dots of light come through your beautiful stained glass, detracting from their overall beauty?

❖ Rattles cause your windows to be "heard before they're seen"?

❖ Cold drafts are driving heating costs unexpectedly higher?

❖ The beauty of your windows has faded?

If you answered *yes* to any of the questions above, it might make sense for us to talk. We are Waters Craftsmen, with more than 20 years of experience solving these problems for beautiful churches like yours.

Call us at 800-123-4567. We love restoring stained glass to its heavenly appearance!

My client received a tremendous response from this one-page letter. Note that client gaps or problems took up most of the page. Features and benefits took up very little space. Remember, the objective of any prospecting activity is to identify prospects who have gaps they want to narrow or close.

Marketing to Your Best Prospects

Before we close this chapter, let's consider the most underutilized prospecting opportunity in many businesses: your existing client base. I won't go into all the reasons companies do such a poor job here. Instead of asking, What else can we sell this client? You should be asking, *What other gaps or problems might our clients have that we can help them with?*

Here's a simple and effective way to begin the process.

1. List every problem you help your clients solve.

2. Ask yourself: How many of our clients are aware that we solve each of these problems? (Probably less than 10 percent!)

3. In a sales meeting, ask your staff to identify instances where they helped clients solve these problems from your list.

4. Develop a success story around each example. This is a story you can share with your clients, when face-to-face, on the phone, or in a client newsletter. Begin the story from the client's experience—the problem or gap they faced, what it was costing them, the additional problems that surfaced, and so forth.

5. You're now prepared to prospect in the most receptive market in your industry—your satisfied client base.

One of the most frustrating experiences you'll experience can occur when an existing client says, *Oh, can you also address that problem? I wish we had known. Just last month we purchased a solution from....*

A small accounting firm I was working with sent out a quarterly client newsletter. In every edition, we added a story about a client problem that they had solved. The story featured client testimonials describing life before and after the gap was closed. Every mailing generated calls from other clients with the same gap who wanted help. As they solved more of their clients' problems, these clients referred them to new clients facing similar gaps. Word-of-mouth advertising is powerful. This approach simply gives your clients the words and stories to use.

A satisfied client is the easiest prospect to sell, because trust, credibility, and relationship are well established. Your clients still have problems, and you are in business to solve them. Perhaps these problems didn't exist a year ago. Perhaps the salesperson or the client overlooked them. Whatever the reason, if the gap is large enough or painful enough, the client will tell you about it. But only if he knows you can help. Spread the word.

Chapter 14

The Psychology of Resistance

Understanding Your Client's Viewpoint

What to do with objections?

Sales organizations invest millions of dollars on seminars and training to better learn how to deal with them, how to confront them, how to feel about them, how to understand them. This can be a good investment, but only if salespeople understand that objections are part of communication, or its absence.

If you ask a salesperson what is involved in becoming a good communicator, you'll probably hear things such as:

* ❖ Speaking clearly and logically
* ❖ Having well organized thoughts planned in advance
* ❖ Maintaining eye contact
* ❖ Ensuring that body language and words are congruent
* ❖ Speaking with confidence

All these skills are important, but they deal with only half of communication—the half that comes from the salesperson. What about the information, feelings, and concerns that come from your client? Good communicators get other people to open up and tell their story. And then they listen. And learn.

How often have you debriefed someone and discovered that the salesperson heard what the client said but not what he really meant? If they miss the meaning beneath the words, how effective has that communication been? If they don't listen effectively, it's usually because most of their attention is caught up in thinking. I don't know who authored the following comment, but it certainly applies to salespeople: *For most people, the opposite of talking is not listening. It's waiting!*

Have you ever observed a salesperson waiting for a client to finish a thought so he could jump in and respond? I've even seen salespeople who couldn't wait. They interrupted the client, tearing down what communication and rapport had been established. Salespeople who are insecure or who need to impress their customers are most often guilty here. Add a dose of poor impulse control, and you have a scenario from childhood: the youngster interrupting grownups because he can't wait to say something "important." Both situations result from a lack of awareness of the other person. It's certainly more forgivable and less damaging when a six-year-old does it, but either situation can actually create resistance from others.

On the other hand, salespeople who are confident and relaxed (operating from their Adult) give clients the time and space to express themselves. They use their Nurturing Parent to encourage more openness and trust. If the client does have a problem, a concern or objection, the salesperson hears (from his Adult) what it is and is in a position to explore what's behind it. He's in no hurry (from his Child) to debate or score points with the client. He's not trying to prove himself right or the client wrong. He knows that in the world of professional selling you rarely prove anything.

Certainly one of the major challenges for most salespeople is learning how to deal with resistance from prospects and clients. At some sales seminars you'll hear trainers and showmen shout:

❖ Prospects will find the following technique irresistible....

❖ With this response your buyer will always say yes....

❖ If you get a price objection, all you need to say is....

You probably felt as insulted as I did. In the real world, people do have objections and offer resistance, and you need to understand why.

What Objections Really Mean

Most resistance has its source in the following:

1. Your client doesn't like something that you've just told or shown him.

2. Your client doesn't understand something you've just told or shown him.

3. You client is uncomfortable (not-OK) with how you've made your point.

4. Some combination of the situations above.

Remember how winners take responsibility for every outcome? Your salespeople need to ask themselves, *What have I done to help create these circumstances?* If they are going to become more capable of handling resistance, they can't blame their clients. No learning or growth will occur as long as there's blaming or excuse-making.

Below are some debriefing questions geared toward resistance salespeople encounter, but they should be asking themselves:

* ❖ At what point did the objection arise?

* ❖ What kind of body language did I notice?

* ❖ What did I do or say immediately beforehand? Was the resistance a response to what I said or how I said it?

* ❖ What exact words and body language did I use?

* ❖ Did it sound like they came from my Critical Parent or my Nurturing Parent?

* ❖ Did I try to refute the objection, or did I try to uncover what was behind it? Did I go for the *why* behind the *what*?

* ❖ Did I respond from my Nurturing Parent?

* ❖ Did I respond from my Adult, using product knowledge?

* ❖ Did my Critical Parent show in my response?

* ❖ How did his body language change after my response?

* ❖ How was I feeling then? Was I feeling helpless, in my Child?

Two Killer Words

Dealing with resistance and what lies behind it is often a delicate issue. Once salespeople get an objection, they often inflict severe damage to themselves by responding with two particular words:

1. But

2. However

Both discount or negate the words, thoughts and feelings that preceded them. They also announce that what follows is the real truth.

Remember this one?

Sam, your company is one of the providers we've always relied on. We like how you handled the numerous requests and changes during the past several months while our various departments had their say. And your final proposal was a good one. However, in this case we've decided to....

It's reminiscent of years past when somebody said:

Sam, I really like you, and I've enjoyed these last two months. We've had a lot of fun together, and you've been a real gentleman. However, I just think it's time that we....

In both cases Sam received strokes (often valid and earned), as if to make up for the fact that he was being shoved out into the world of also-rans.

You certainly don't want your clients feeling this way from your comments. The words but and however, used in the wrong way, can ruin your day. If your client offers an objection to the price you've just quoted, it's a mistake to reply,

Helen, our price is high. However, I'm sure that when you consider....

By using "however," you've just told Helen that she was wrong! If you were watching Helen, you noticed that she just became defensive or was ready to attack. Instead of being open and receptive, she's prepared for a fight—or at best a debate. You've put Helen in a not-OK position, and she will see you as the cause of her not-OKness. You've created trouble for yourself.

Let's try a different approach by using the word "and."

Helen, you're right—our price is high. And you told me that last year when you bought from a lower-priced supplier, their system had some flaws that slowed down your response in time-critical situations. Can we discuss this trade-off so I can understand more completely where your priorities are?

As I mentioned earlier, our objective is not to debate Helen or to prove her wrong. We want to work with her to arrive at an informed buying decision that solves her problems without creating new ones. Like all buyers Helen has values, and they are usually based on her beliefs and experiences. Our goal is to uncover values, her beliefs and her experiences, so we can direct our efforts in an appropriate direction.

There are other psychological considerations here. First, if we tell Helen that she's wrong in her views, she'll resist. Nobody wants to feel as if they're losing out to a salesperson. That would represent an extremely not-OK position for a buyer. Second, Helen doesn't want to feel manipulated like a puppet on a string. One technique that's still be taught today to deal with prices objections is the response,

"You're right, our price is high. Is that the only reason you hesitate going ahead with a 'yes' decision today?"

Who wouldn't feel manipulated by that kind of move? This ancient technique (designed to isolate the objection) is an attempt to ensure this objection is the only one left, so the salesperson can "close on it." In reality, the prospect feels like she's been put into a corner and the only way out is to give up her wallet to the salesperson. Prospects are highly unlikely to respond candidly to such an overtly manipulative, condescending tactic. These kinds of techniques don't work on today's sophisticated buyers, and I doubt they were ever very effective. They almost announce to the client, *I'm gonna win and get your money.* Don't be surprised if when one of your salespeople tries this approach, the client challenges, "Where did you learn that old move?"

If you want to uncover whether the price objection is the only barrier left, try a response that doesn't threaten Helen with not-OKness: "Helen, you're right. And I get the feeling that even if our price was more in line with what you were expecting, there would still be other things standing in our way...yes?"

Let's understand the psychology at work here:

1. Using our Nurturing Parent, we've agreed with Helen, allowing her to maintain her OKness. She may even drop her defenses a bit.

2. By using the word *and* instead of *but* or *however*, we haven't announced that we're about to prove Helen wrong. She is still in OK territory as we continue with our response.

3. Instead of pushing her into a corner as we try to uncover whether or not price is the only obstacle to doing business, we've taken an approach that actually backs away from her. The reverse psychology we've introduced stands a better chance of uncovering the truth, because Helen doesn't feel threatened or manipulated. Her defenses are further lowered as she relaxes.

You might ask: Isn't this approach just as manipulative as the old style, aggressive move we just dismissed? Well, yes. And it's more effective because the client won't recognize it. Instead, with this approach Helen is likely to respond either with a "yes" or a "no." If she admits that there are other problems you need to resolve, you'll take note of them. If she has a substantial laundry list of objections, you're unlikely to do business, but at least you haven't fought the price justification battle with someone who has already made up her mind. If Helen says there isn't anything else standing in the way, you can pursue the discussion further. Often she'll tell you that she has a lower price/bid from a competitor.

At this point, you may want to introduce the Values Triangle we discussed in the previous chapter. You can judge whether you want to draw it on paper, or just talk about it. One soft way to introduce a values discussion is to ask, "If our price was more in line with that of the competitor you just mentioned, which one do you think you'd be favoring?"

If she favors your competitor, you have no chance, because you've lost at multiple points on the triangle. But if she says, "Oh, all things being equal, we'd prefer to go with you."

It's time to smile, thank her for her candor, and ask nicely, "Why?"

She'll most likely tell you what she prefers about your solution and your company. These are your competitive advantages. Coming from her, they're valid considerations. Those same statements out of your mouth constitute a sales pitch, and they will carry less weight and validity in her mind. You can then develop the values triangle further, heading toward the conclusion that you get what you pay for. I find that a value equation comparison is a powerful tool in these instances.

On paper it will look like:

$$\frac{\text{Our price}}{\text{Their price}} = \frac{\text{All of our competitive advantages}}{\text{Their competitive disadvantages}}$$

After developing this picture in Helen's mind, you can ask (from your Nurturing Parent), "Helen, based on what you've just told me about your priorities, does our pricing seem any more justified?"

Although this chapter isn't intended to be a manual on sales technique, I want to emphasize the importance of the psychological impact, for better or worse, of any tactics your salespeople use. Antiquated sales techniques—you can learn them from almost any sales book more than 25 years old, and sadly some even more recent—tend to have a negative psychological impact on the customer, as well as on your chances of success. It's unfortunate that some of these techniques are still being taught today, and innocent salespeople learn them at their peril.

If You Sell

❖ If you don't consider the psychological impact of any technique you use, you run the risk of losing not only a sale but also a customer.

❖ You can't evaluate the impact of any technique until you experience it from the mind of a customer. Role-playing a scenario from both sides is essential.

❖ Top sales professionals understand and respect their client's point of view, without necessarily buying into it.

When I debrief salespeople and they tell me what they said to a customer, I often ask them, *How would you feel if somebody said that to you?* Usually they get my point. After all, a technique is simply a practical method applied to accomplish a task more efficiently. If any sales technique hinders your progress, it's probably having a negative psychological effect on your customer as well. And the opposite is of course true—if you create a negative psychological or emotional situation for your customer, he won't reward you by buying.

I've seen very few selling approaches with a firm psychological basis, and I believe that this why salespeople have so much trouble using what they've learned from most sales books and seminars. What sounds exciting in a seminar doesn't translate into the real sales world unless the strategies and tactics take into consideration how clients will react to them. One of your many management responsibilities is to ensure that your staff is skilled in these dynamics. You should be asking them:

❖ How would you feel if somebody said that to you?

❖ If a salesperson used that tone, would it bring you closer to agreement, or turn you off?

❖ If you were asked that question, would you feel OK or not-OK?

❖ Does that question sound like it's coming from his Critical Parent or his Nurturing Parent? What effect is it having?

Exercise

At a sales meeting you'll play the client and offer the following statements, to which your sales staff must respond without using *but* or *however*, and still make their point or ask a relevant question.

1. I've heard ABC Co. has a new methodology that has everyone else playing catch up.

2. This is far more than we had budgeted.

3. Smith Co. seems to be stronger in the technical support department than your company.

4. Why do so many companies overpromise and then underdeliver when it comes to this problem?

5. As you may know, we worked with your company four years ago in this area, and due to some significant problems you couldn't resolve, we aren't optimistic about another try.

And, of course, you can insert objections and statements from your own experience.

Chapter 15

The Psychology of Persuasion

Getting to Know You

George, a salesperson, has just left Janet's office, shaking his head. Janet wasn't really engaged in his presentation, and he can't understand why. Here is George's summary of what happened: *After she briefed me on what she was looking for, I gave her a quick overview of our company and how we could provide the best solution for her. I told her the story of how the competition's top two customers had switched to us and how satisfied they've been. Janet did ask several questions, and we covered a tremendous amount of specifics. But when I asked her for a decision, she shut down. Then I asked her what it was going to take to do business, and she said, "More time to evaluate." I know she understands how strong our solution is compared to the others she's seen. The story I told always works. What's wrong with her?*

Who was George really selling to here? Did he really understand his client? George is typical of many salespeople who tend to sell everybody the same way.

Remember the Golden Rule? *Do unto others, as you would have them do unto you.* To George this means, *Sell people the way you want to be sold. Present to people the way you want to be presented to.*

And this works perfectly well…as long as these people are exactly like you! But what if they aren't? If we are going to succeed in influencing customers, we are going to have to make some adjustments to the Golden Rule. In business, we must translate it as: *Do unto others, as they want to be done unto. Sell people the way they want to be sold. Present to people the way they want to be presented to.*

After all, because lively stories impress you, will they impress the next client you call on? If you appreciate lots of details that provide a context and structure for understanding the main thrust of an idea, does that mean your next client wants to learn this way? If you don't think small talk has any value in warming up a conversation before you get down to business, does that mean your next client will agree? If you enjoy getting to the bottom line quickly, does that mean the next prospect you call on is comfortable moving this quickly?

We're all different. The most costly mistake salespeople make is to overlook this fact, because they then present just as they would like to be presented to. I call this operating on autopilot, or selling to yourself. It can prove both dangerous and costly. George gave his standard presentation; Janet wasn't impressed, and the result was the delay or loss of a sale. Although professional selling has many different elements, surely communication is ranks near the top in importance.

☞ Key Thoughts

❖ We like people like us.

❖ We prefer to buy from people we like.

❖ If you want people to like and buy from you, be like them.

One of the most costly mistakes that people make is to think that people think like them. Think about it!

Typically salespeople don't strategize how to apply the third bullet point, so they slip up on the fourth. They've overlooked the psychological side of professional selling. To make sure this doesn't continue with your sales staff, let's consider some ways people express themselves. We'll be using a model developed at Harvard's Business School in the 1960's. I was first introduced to this model in 1978 by sales trainer Stan Smith. Since then I've read or heard versions from other trainers, including Charles Clarke, Roger Dawson, Tony Alessandra, Kurt Mortensen, Stephen Schiffman, Marguerite Smolen and others. What follows is a version that you can easily teach and incorporate into your overall selling strategy.

Consider the two lines below. The first measures how directly people express themselves.

Indirect————————————————————**Direct**

slower paced	fast paced
less assertive	more assertive
less competitive	more competitive
more cooperative	less cooperative
more of a team player	more independent
reserved in comments	more outspoken
cautious in decisions	shoots from the hip
makes points by building up slowly	gets to point quickly
sees and talks about shades of gray	black-and-white opinions
speaks more slowly	speaks quickly
avoids risks	risk-taker
rule follower	will bend rules
moves at others' pace	impatient
you may have to read between the lines to uncover true intent	you never doubt what they mean
focused on the process	wants results quickly
asks	tells

Now consider three people you know reasonably well, either from your career or from your personal life. It's highly unlikely that any of them exhibits all the qualities in one column and none of those in the other column. What's more likely is that people you know exhibit more qualities from one column than from the other. These people are clearly either direct or indirect in the way they express themselves. By the way, if you are more indirect, do you find that those clients who are more direct tend to make you feel not-OK?

Now let's look at these same three people on another line: openness, which is a measure of how much of themselves they reveal when they speak.

Contained————————————————————————Open	
more reserved at first	friendly, animated
more poker-faced	read them like a book
reveal themselves on a need to know basis	open up quickly and share personals
makes friends on own terms	easy to get to know
decisions by reason, logic facts	gut feelings, intuition, emotions
cool, guarded at first	warm from the beginning
clock-watcher	flexible about time
avoids small talk	small talk before business
taskoriented	relationship-oriented
detail-oriented	details can be omitted
loves precision	close can be acceptable
prove it to me	explain it to me
make it logical	make it interesting

Again, these three people are unlikely to have all the qualities in one column and none in the other. But aren't they clearly open or contained? If you find yourself at one extreme, do you find those clients on the other extreme are the tough ones to relate to and communicate with?

Now let's rotate the contained/open line 90 degrees clockwise, and then we'll superimpose it on the indirect/direct line, as follows:

Remember plane geometry from eighth or ninth grade, with the X-axis and Y-axis? (Don't worry, there won't be a test.) I've chosen three people for this exercise, and we'll plot them on the graph above. Let's assume they are:

1. George-who is extremely direct and about halfway open.

2. Leslie-who is half way indirect and half way contained.

3. Angie—who is extremely indirect and extremely open.

From these descriptions I've placed them at the

appropriate points on the graph below.

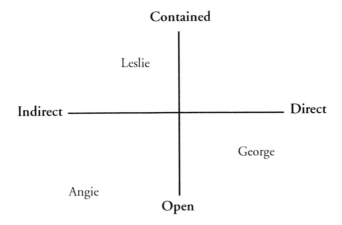

Now we'll label the four quadrants so we can more easily identify and use them.

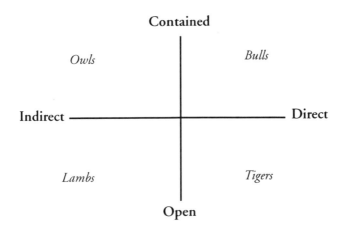

Some 2,500 years ago Chinese general Sun Tzu wrote *The Art of War*, which contains not only timeless military strategy (it's required reading for our future military leaders at West Point Academy), but also wisdom on how to live successfully in society. He uses the term shih (pronounced "shir") to describe the ability to know how things are in the world, how they work together and how to subtly influence them at the right time for greater harmony. Shih is used to attain a goal without generating confrontation and conflict. This is precisely our objective when selling, and a useful method is to identify our client's personality and then adapt our behavior to mirror his. We subtly move into their quadrant so they are more comfortable (OK) with us. (Remember, they tend to like people like them.)

As we describe these four personalities and how best to deal with them, keep in mind that nobody inhabits only one quadrant all the time—everyone is a combination of all four. Usually however, one or perhaps two styles will predominate. For example, on the previous chart George may find himself in the Tiger or the Bull quadrants, depending on the situation. He's clearly direct, whether he's more focused on the task (contained) or the relationship (open).

First let's consider the **Bulls**, also referred to as dominant directors or aggressives, because they sometimes show more Critical Parent when expressing themselves. When dealing with them, here are some points to keep in mind:

1. Be precise, organized, and disciplined in your presentation.

2. Unless they tell you otherwise, keep the conversation focused on business—their targets and goals, not yours.

3. Demonstrate bottom-line results and benefits with associated costs.

4. Phrases like "return on investment" and "bottom line" get their attention because that's the way they process things.

5. Always give them the gift of time: If you have 30 minutes for your meeting, take no more than 27.

6. Since they tend to have a black and white view of the world, don't express your ideas in a fuzzy or wishy-washy fashion.

7. Bulls respect power and confidence, so be bold—even courageous—in your statements (as long as you can back them up).

8. They like explanations short and to the point, so don't give too much detail in your answers. It's better to ask a Bull if he or she needs more detail than to dive right into the bits and bytes in your explanation.

9. They like to measure by previous results, so your track record should be strong and relevant.

10. Be prepared to answer questions, because they like having control and want information now.

11. Inefficiency and indecision tend to irritate them. If you waffle or appear unsure, you can blow the sale even when your solution is superior.

12. They won't hesitate to tell you if they don't like what you're telling/showing them. Don't take it personally, because they're just expressing themselves in the way they're comfortable.

13. Which personality has the most trouble selling to Bulls? It's the Lambs—who have little in common with them (they're positioned directly opposite them on the graph). Owls at least are focused efficiently on the task, and Tigers at least can speak directly to them. On the other hand, Owls often move too slowly and appear indecisive to Bulls. Tigers

often talk too much and stray from the bottom line for them. Lambs are intimidated by Bulls and often have to stretch far outside their comfort zone to reach them. Lambs need to practice and role-play direct questions and explanations before calling on Bulls.

14. When they're selling, Bulls tend to overwhelm and steamroll Lambs if they aren't careful. Bulls can sometimes come across as pushy and uncaring, forcing others into a not-OK position.

15. Bulls can sound authoritative because they are direct and strong in their statements. This doesn't mean they know more than anybody else. Always separate what they say from how they say it to avoid drawing the wrong conclusion.

Because they live in their Adult ego state, **Owls** are the cautious thinkers or analyticals of the group. Making an informed, objective decision through an efficient evaluation process makes sense to them. Here are some points to keep in mind when selling to Owls:

1. Your briefing should be rational, logical, systematic, and even predictable. You might want to begin your meeting by asking the Owl what he'd like to learn from you. You can explain: "My objective is to provide enough information so you can make an informed decision and secure the best solution for your organization."

2. You will need valid evidence to support any statements you make. Owls dislike and discount sweeping generalizations, so avoid using them. Don't exaggerate.

3. Owls tend to be private, and they view their space as their own. Don't touch anything on an Owl's desk without permission.

4. Always provide best case and worst case scenarios for

any decision outcomes. Owls want a balanced, objective presentation so they can compare and contrast more easily. If your approach is too obviously slanted or biased, they will tend to reject it as invalid. Conversely, if they see your approach as sincerely balanced and informative, they are more likely to embrace your conclusions.

5. More than the other personality styles Owls distrust salespeople. They often complain that salespeople don't know what they're talking about. Make sure you do. Before calling on them, brush up on your facts and decide which ones to use in your discussion. Make sure you're organized!

6. Don't ever try to force a decision with an Owl. Give them facts, data, and more statistics so they can arrive at their conclusions deliberately after weighing all the evidence and checking it several times. If you match their deliberate pace, they'll feel more comfortable.

7. With Owls you'll probably need to go into more detail and depth than you're used to in your explanations (sorry, Tigers). If you are naturally direct, be patient with them. Stay with a point or detail as long as they want. It's the Owl who calls you and says, "I'd like to go over a point on your proposal just one more time. On page 3, paragraph IV, point 7, the phrase 'is likely to result in'; I would like additional projections from your accounting department so I can understand the precise implications here. When do you think I will be able to get this data from you?" Close your eyes, focus your awareness on your breathing, and smile before you respond.

8. If an Owl asks you a question you can't answer, don't get defensive, and above all don't try to fake it. Admit what you don't know and promise to find the answer (and do it!) in an acceptable time frame. If an Owl catches you in an exaggeration or false claim, he will immediately become

suspicious, asking themselves, what else should I mistrust? You risk losing credibility if you're caught exaggerating.

9. Since Owls seek precision and enjoy details, you won't be effective with phrases like, *probably, perhaps, chances are, most likely, there's a possibility that.* When an Owl hears a term like most likely, he's thinking, Does that mean there's a 51 percent or 93 percent chance of happening? Without more specific data, an Owl can become uncomfortable. A more persuasive approach with an Owl is to state, "65 percent of clients responding to our June survey reported that their downtime was reduced more than 25 percent over the previous year. Although we're pleased with this data, we also know that 35 percent did not have this experience. That's why we continue to invest 20 percent of our gross profits in research and development."

10. Since Owls are indirect, they avoid confrontation. This means they may not come right out and tell you, No! if they don't like your solution. Instead, they will continue to ask you pointed questions, often ending with something like, I'm not sure that you've completely proven your case that you can deliver the benefits you're claiming for the stated investment on our part. Do you have any additional evidence I could review?

11. Owls are focused on practicalities like savings of time and money, measured improvements in quality or customer retention, reductions in downtime that translate into greater profitability per worker hour.

12. Owls don't want to be embarrassed. Any time they are shown to be wrong, you should quickly advise them that this is a common but insignificant mistake. Then you can ask them a question that gives them an opportunity to demonstrate their knowledge or expertise. You never want them to see you as responsible for their not-OKness.

13. If an Owl feels pressure from you, he'll withdraw from the conversation. You can bring them back by asking a question that again allows them to display their knowledge.

14. Owls like to be left alone to do their work and make their decisions. They won't consider making a buying decision in the company of somebody who is trying to sell them.

15. It's the Tigers—directly opposite them on the graph-who are continuously frustrated when selling to Owls. Tigers naturally sell with emotion, stories and examples that are short on facts and proof. They move forward so quickly that Owls get uncomfortable, feeling steamrolled. I've met numerous Owls who can't understand why Tigers sell them as they do—Owls aren't comfortable buying that way.

16. Since so many salespeople fall into the Tiger category, and since so many technical buyers are Owls, this presents a major challenge. If you don't know how to adjust to the Owl's style, you'll be continually frustrated. And lose selling opportunities.

17. An increasing number of owls are now in sales. Although they don't tend to make great prospectors—most are too contained/introverted for this—they do communicate effectively with other Owls who are technical buyers. The high-tech boom has seen a migration of Owls from product specialist to sales engineer to full-fledged sales professional.

Lambs are also known as steady relaters and supporters. They are well liked because their Nurturing Parent is naturally at work. If you're selling to Lambs, you'll want to remember the following points:

1. The more direct you naturally are, the more important it is for you to slow down with Lambs. Show you're interested

in them as a person, not just a sale. Take time to listen to their concerns and their aspirations. Don't let them see you checking your watch.

2. If you must disagree, don't debate facts. Instead, let them know how you feel about the situation: *I can see your point here. I've found that other alternatives are also worth considering, such as....*

3. Lambs need to see you as sincerely caring about their concerns and their organization or team. Any solution you offer should address the effects it will have on everyone involved. They love solutions that improve morale or teamwork. They like ideas that their staff or company can easily buy into or adopt. *User friendly* has special importance for them.

4. Lambs like solutions that don't rock the boat. If you can show them that you'll hold everyone's hand along the way—during the installation phase, for example—they are more likely to embrace your solution: *I see it as my responsibility to stay with you and your team throughout the installation process, so if questions or concerns arise, I'm there to help. This is what I would want if I were in your shoes.* Lambs should see you as the ultimate team player.

5. Closing the sale should be soft, gentle, and indirect: *Jim, it seems to me that your entire organization would greatly benefit from faster response time. One byproduct we've see is that employees often feel better about the job they're doing as their customers are more satisfied. This can do wonders for company morale. How do you see the situation?*

6. Since Lambs enjoy being of service and helping others, if they see you in this way their comfort level will increase.

7. Because Lambs don't like confrontation, they may not raise many objections. *This does not mean* they are buying

what you are selling! They will often give you a compliment (stroke) instead of a decision, especially if they aren't necessarily convinced: *I can see some very interesting applications here. I'm certainly going to make sure the other managers have an opportunity to hear about this.* Don't read this as a green light. Lambs don't like telling you *No!* They'd rather maintain a good relationship and avoid any arm-wrestling, so they're less likely to raise objections. They don't want pressure.

8. If a Lamb does bother to raise an objection, you must realize that it's vitally important to them since they'd rather avoid any confrontation.

9. A good strategy with Lambs is to let them know up front that it's OK for them to tell you *No!* if that's how they feel: *Bill, if you should come to the conclusion that we don't have a fit, I just want you to feel comfortable telling me. No hard feelings, OK?* This allows them to feel comfortable telling you the truth, instead of having to mislead you and lengthen your selling cycle. Unless you use this kind of up-front strategy, Lambs may allow you to make repeated sales calls on them, even when they have no intention of buying.

Tigers, the natural extroverts in the group, are also called interactive socializers. If you're selling to Tigers, note the following:

1. Stimulating conversation appeals to them. Don't be too quiet or reserved in your comments. They like to talk, especially about themselves. Note any personal comments they make, so they'll be favorably impressed when you bring them up later.

2. Caution: although they enjoy adventurous and exciting conversation, this doesn't mean they're buying your solution.

A lively meeting with a Tiger doesn't always translate into a sale.

3. Analogies, stories, examples, and name-dropping will make your points more effectively than detailed, logical proofs.

4. Once you reach agreement, you *must* reassure Tigers you will be with them at every step to take care of details, which they tend to overlook. *Mike, one area where we excel is staying on top of all the details, so nothing falls through the cracks. Because you have more important things to deal with, we sweat the small stuff.* If you allow them to enjoy the glory of the solution without the details, they will become loyal clients.

5. Ask them open-ended questions about their goals and even their dreams: *Tell me, what kinds of things will you do with the profits from this investment? How will management view this program if we can help you hit your target of reducing emissions by 25 percent?*

6. Since they tend to be less interested in details, you can be effective with terms such as "probably," "there's a good chance that," "most likely," "many of our best clients enjoy," and so forth. (These are the phrases that annoy Owls—in the opposite quadrant.)

7. Tigers want to make a good impression on their peers and their management. If your solution increases the chances of this happening, they are likely to embrace it. If your solution involves a high risk of them looking bad or losing prestige, they will reject it.

8. Many Tigers have a short attention span—they're interested in what you have to say, but not for long. This may be one reason why they tend to be more of an impulse buyer than other personalities. They can buy a good story,

told by a good storyteller, and later regret it.

When debriefing salespeople, you should ask them, *What personality are we dealing with? Is she more direct or indirect? Is she more open or contained?* Ask these questions first, before you ask whether the client is a Bull, Owl, Lamb, or Tiger. It's more likely your salespeople can identify where the client is on only one axis rather than both. This is especially true if it's a first meeting.

In fall 2000 I was referred to a training and development director of a large media company in New York. Within the first five minutes of my initial phone call, I learned she was a liberal democrat living on the Upper West Side, and her sister was very active in Al Gore's presidential campaign. This information was *not* the result of any great questioning skills on my part; it came solely from how open she was. People really do reveal themselves to you—if you know how to listen and what to listen for.

You can role-play selling to the different personality styles in your sales meetings. Your staff can take turns responding to a price objection, explaining how a program works, or asking a qualifying question with each style. It makes for lively discussions and effective learning.

Potholes in the Road Ahead

Below are some common selling situations where salespeople on autopilot tend to stumble:

1. When a Tigers/Lambs (both open) selling to Owls/Bulls (both contained) spend too much time on small talk or asking personal questions, they can create not-OK feelings in the client.

2. Bulls/Tigers, focusing on quick results, may not listen patiently enough to Owls/Lambs (process-oriented) and come across as pushy, uncaring or aggressive.

3. Lambs can sound indecisive and wimpy to Bulls if they spend too much time on processes and procedures before getting to the bottom line.

4. Owls can bore Tigers with a logical, step-by-step thought process filled only with facts.

5. Tigers can appear disorganized and unprepared when selling to Owls.

You'll be able to identify examples of these situations from a review of yours staff's last several weeks of client interactions. You can't fix the past, but you can resolve not to repeat it.

By the way...remember Janet and George from the beginning of this chapter? Who were they? Let's start with George, the sales rep: He focused—or attempted to—on the big picture, skirting the details, trying to impress Janet with his story about the competition's customer who became his client. Isn't that like a Tiger...a Tiger who was on autopilot, selling to himself?

Now consider Janet: She asked a lot of questions about specifics, wasn't impressed by George's story, and shut down when George asked her for a decision, using her standard request for more information. She's an Owl, and George moved too quickly for her. His first and biggest mistake was focusing on his presentation to the exclusion of his prospect.

🖝 Key Thoughts

❖ If you don't know and use the Golden Rule of business communication, you're selling to yourself. And you may be the only one who buys!

❖ Do unto others, as they want to be done unto. Sell others they way they want to be sold.

❖ Generic presentations are rarely persuasive. Customize every presentation to fit your prospect.

If You Sell

❖ Understanding whom you're selling to is at least as important as what you're selling. Become an expert in personalities. From this day forward, *no more generic presentations!*

❖ Want to have fun with these concepts? Whenever you talk with prospects, clients or acquaintances, see how quickly you can determine where they are on the two lines: Open/Contained and the Direct/Indirect.

❖ In your contact management system, have a line next to the client name that reads: D/I O/C; B O L T. Circle the appropriate descriptions and then review them before each phone call or meeting.

Exercise

Have different staff members play a Bull, Owl, Lamb, or Tiger and offer objections. The others offer replies appropriate to the personality style.

You can also have different people express the same objection from each personality style. Others will reply accordingly.

As you master these concepts and strategies, you are

becoming what Sun Tzu calls a skillful warrior—one who wins battles without having to fight them. Victory is gained not from defeating, but from influencing through subtle means. It's the way of the skillful warrior, and the true sales professional.

Management Applications

As you might imagine, these concepts and strategies can be fundamental to your success in communicating with your individual salespeople. Some questions to ask yourself before having that next meeting with a member of your sales team:

❖ With what personality am I dealing?

❖ What's the most effective way for me to convey my message, so it's most likely to be heard?

❖ How should I ask for commitment from this person?

❖ Based on his personality, how much time should I allow for this meeting?

❖ Will I need to demonstrate more patience than normal with this person?

❖ Will this person need to show more patience with me than he's used to?

☛ Key Thought

❖ Don't go into a meeting with anyone without first considering the personalities with which you will have to communicate.

Chapter 16

Where Do I Go From Here?

And in What Order?

You haven't read this book in one sitting. I hope you've tried some of the strategies and interventions along the way. If you haven't yet done much with what you've been reading, you're probably wondering, where do I start?

You always start from where you are and with what resources—people and time—you have. What follows is not a sequential road map, because your mix of people and problems is unique. Having said that, below are some keys to translating this book into a dynamic process of personal and professional growth for your entire sales staff.

Let's start with the big picture. You now have a more in depth understanding of your salespeople, their customers, what happens between them and why. You have identified the causes of many problems individual salespeople have, and know what to do about them.

Below is a generic sequence, which you can rearrange as you see fit...

❖ Introduce your staff to the TA model so they can better understand what's holding them back (chapters 1 through 3).

❖ Start coaching and debriefing those salespeople who have real potential for growth (chapter 7).

❖ Stop buying excuses now (chapter 6).

❖ If you have people with high need for approval, address it and decide together if they will do what it takes to grow out of it (chapter 2).

❖ If you have individuals whose production has leveled off, help them set goals (chapter 10).

❖ Turn your sales meetings into sales psychology workshops on personality styles, prospecting, resistance, selling, and buying (chapters 11 through 15).

❖ Role-play constantly.

❖ And last but perhaps first in importance: Enjoy growing your people and your revenues!

About the Author

Mark Wilensky, president of High Mark Systems, is a sales development expert with 30 years experience in a wide variety of industries. His unique psychological approach to building selling and sales management systems is matched by his dynamic presentation style. A featured speaker at industry sales and association meetings, he brings a rare combination of humor, penetrating insights and powerful strategies that captivate audiences. His unique ability to get into the minds of customers and prospects turns selling challenges into win-win partnerships.

For more information about his programs you can contact him at Markwilensky.com. or at 301/854-2585

CPSIA information can be obtained at www.ICGtesting.com
Printed in the USA
BVOW031334130612

292572BV00002B/115/P